LISA CROFT lives in Lancashire and was a lil
She writes this account on behalf of her mc
who was born when her father was imprisoned in Spain, anu ..
Jennifer Talavera Williams, who is named after that Spanish jail's location.

WILLY MALEY teaches at the University of Glasgow and is co-author, with his brother John, of *From the Calton to Catalonia*, a play based around their father's experiences in Spain in 1937.

JENNIE RENTON is a secondhand bookseller and publishing freelancer in her home city of Edinburgh. As founder-editor of *Scottish Book Collector* she produced over 80 issues of the magazine; she also edited *Folio* for the National Library of Scotland.

TAM WATTERS worked as a coal miner for 25 years until Bilston Glen Colliery closed. A keen amateur photographer, he went on to work as a camera sales adviser for the next 23 years and is now retired. In his younger days he was a Scottish weightlifting champion.

All royalties generated from the sale of this book will be donated to the International Brigade Memorial Trust (IBMT) which 'keeps alive the memory and spirit of the men and women who fought fascism in Spain from 1936 to 1939'. www.international-brigades.org.uk

Praise for *Our Fathers Fought Franco*:

A landmark work [that] reads like a detective novel, slowly uncovering the traumatic experience that all four men were reluctant to describe in later life. These events are set in the context of whole lives... Spain was the revolution they wanted at home... An unforgettable, essential book.
—ANGUS REID, THE MORNING STAR

Such openness connects us readers to the vulnerabilities of a family, life in all its complexity and difficulty. This is a virtue of all four accounts in Our Fathers Fought Franco... *What comes through persistently is a sense of how much we have to learn from the past.*—ALAN RIACH, THE NATIONAL

Their stories are of men who understood that the working-class struggle, the fight for fair play, justice and decency, is international. A miner brutalised by the military in Spain's Astorias is the brother-in arms of miners suffering wage cuts in a colliery in Glasgow, Nottingham or South Wales. Maley, Renton, Watters and Williams, each to different degrees, were beaten, wounded, imprisoned and never once did they lose sight of their beliefs and mission. Each story is moving, carefully considered and makes you want to sit down in a pub and have a drink with those men who set out to make a difference and did so.—CLIFFORD THURLOW

The four men were captured on 13 February 1937. They witnessed several of their comrades being executed and were then lined up to be shot. Fortunately, at this point the fascists realised the men were British and wanted them alive to use as a bargaining tool, so the executions were halted, and they were subsequently freed as part of a prisoner exchange.
—ANDY GRAHAM, ASLEF JOURNAL

After just five weeks' training, they literally jumped out of a lorry into the frontline of the battle at Jarama... This book deserves to be read and treasured.—CHRIS BAMBERY, COUNTERFIRE

Part first-person history, part war memoir, part working-class polemic, it is a valuable addition to the canon.—RICHARD BATH, SCOTTISH FIELD

Our Fathers Fought Franco

James Maley, Donald Renton, Geordie Watters
and AC Williams

Edited by

WILLY MALEY

Luath Press Limited

EDINBURGH

www.luath.co.uk

First published 2023

ISBN 978-1-804250-40-2

The paper used in this book is recyclable. It is made
from low chlorine pulps produced in a low energy,
low emission manner from renewable forests.

Printed and bound by
Robertson Printers, Forfar

Typeset in 11 point Sabon LT Pro by
Main Point Books, Edinburgh

Contents

To the International Brigaders and their families

Foreword

THE TENEMENT DOORWAYS of Scottish cities whisper ghosts' names as you pass. Here lived the Robertsons, declare letters engraved on wizened green buzzer plaques, the Patersons and the Crollas too. If you are lucky, their pulling handles are still in place, bulbous and resembling the tops of old police truncheons. Most have disappeared – smelted in the war effort? stolen? – and there is only a small surprised mouth hole.

Whatever their state, it is an enjoyable, diverting pastime to glance at them and speculate as you walk on by – was FRASER a friend of THOMSON? Did NOWAK and DI ROLLO swap stories of immigrant life?

Not so many streets from mine is one such square plaque. J RUSSELL, it reads, and it belonged to an International Brigader. Strolling by this one, at 18 Edina Place in Leith, I do not have so many gaps to fill or flights of fancy to board. I know that one day in 1937, RUSSELL stepped down from this communal entrance, turned left and then left again onto Easter Road, and went to fight in Spain.

My possession of a list that contained the addresses of Scots at the time they volunteered to join the war in Spain domesticated them. They were still remote heroes brimming with courage alien to our times, and yet now I could picture them whistling 'The Internationale' while walking to the grocer's shop or sitting on a park bench reading the *Daily Worker*. It humanised these hitherto otherworldly titans. Another local, Andrew Foley, listed his address as 'Hibs Supporters Club, 72 Easter Road'. I began to think more about their lives before 1936 and after 1939, and most of all about those they left behind or would later bring into the world. To go to Spain you had to have a big heart. You probably knew, then, what it was to love and be loved.

I thought first of the women left here. Strictly speaking, there was a long stage when married men were not supposed to volunteer for the British Battalion of the International Brigade. That edict did not stop some and besides, even in the mid-to-late 1930s, romance blossomed way before it carried couples down the aisle. Occasionally in letters sent home from the Spanish frontline, talk would turn tender and absent hearts come to the fore. Having read these lines, I left them among the pages they were written on, keeping sweet nothings private as they should be, but never forgot them.

Sometimes, if rarely, there would be words from beyond those tenement buzzers – women writing to or about their Brigader loves. My own heart thudded densely when I encountered the words of Mrs C Fry, relaying the story of her recently killed Brigader husband, Harold, a shoemaker from Craigmillar in Edinburgh:

> My husband went to Spain because he realised the danger of fascism and believed that his military experience could best be used in fighting it. He joined the International Brigades because he thought it was the job he could do best. His experience of fascist methods of warfare and their brutal treatment of prisoners behind the lines only helped to strengthen his determination to carry on the fight until Franco, Hitler and Mussolini were beaten. This is why he went back to Spain again after a short period of leave, his wound hardly healed, and without ever seeing his baby boy which was born the day after he left. I would not have stopped him even if I could, because I believe he was right, and I'm sure his last thoughts must have been of regret that he could not live to see the final triumph of the forces he fought for.

'Without ever seeing his baby boy which was born the day after he left' – it is hard to think of a sadder short story. Thoughts of women, then, unravelled into thoughts of children too.

Then I thought of other relatives – brothers and sisters in a familial rather than comradely way, and mums and dads and grandparents. All of them must have worried themselves nauseous. The men's actions bred both pride and resistance, sometimes within the same household.

Three members of the Murray family – Annie, George and Tom – went to Spain; she to nurse and they to fight. Five further sisters were left at home, all campaigning for the Spanish cause and in most cases attempting to serve themselves. The words of one of them, Margaret, summarised the anguish of many remaining here when she spread news of a letter from Annie: 'Annie was in very good spirits and not a bit worried about going out to the fighting zone. Of course, it is much worse for the people left at home, isn't it?'

Less enthused were the uncles of Glaswegian volunteer John Dunlop. Learning that John was about to flee his accountancy apprenticeship and travel by rail to Spain, they raced to Central Station to prevent him from taking the early train to Euston. Unfortunately for them, he had already boarded the sleeper service.

In the mid-2000s, I found myself in front of another door and another buzzer. The location now was Riddrie, north-east Glasgow, and the home a neat and clearly cherished semi-detached house. This doorbell worked, a figure emerged behind the frosted panels and I swear her smile permeated through the opaque glass. 'Come away in, son,' said the figure, Nan Park. 'The kettle's on and there's cakes and pieces.' Here was the opposite of Morningside's 'You'll have had your tea.'

Nan was a lifelong socialist as was her husband, George. His father, Alec, had fought in Spain. George sat in his chair – and don't all men of a certain age need *their* chair? – and looked over while wearing the kind of grin which makes you feel as safe as a sleeping cat. He beckoned me to the sofa next to him. 'Has Nan offered you a tea, son?'

Soon, George was a boy again. It was August 1938. He, his brother Eric and their mum, Annie, were in Glasgow City Hall talking to a giant named Paul Robeson. The great American singer had just given a typically invigorating performance during a benefit concert for the Spanish cause. Robeson had, earlier that year, travelled to Spain and met with members of the British Battalion. He distinctly remembered encountering Alec Park. This was why he appeared so upset when informed that Alec had recently been killed in battle. Robeson had a tear in his eye. So too, right now, did George. The Battalion had lost a member; he and Eric had lost much more.

There would be more sons and daughters of Brigaders as I continued to research what became *Homage to Caledonia*. They helped endlessly with details and narratives, of course, but much more importantly, they told me what these men were really like and how they laughed and moved. They made black and white photos colourful and gave accents to letters written three-quarters of a century earlier. They illuminated those years of their fathers' lives prior to the Spanish Civil War and after it – if their dads had come home. And they talked about the legacy of Spain in their own lives and family relationships, good and bad.

Now, when I think of Scottish International Brigaders, I think of their families too. I see the pain of Allan Craig, unable to rest easily until he could find the remains of his father, slain at the Battle of Jarama. I see Tommy

Bloomfield's daughter, telling me how hunger behind the lines in Spain bred in her dad a lifelong habit of eating onions as if they were apples. I see the pride in the eyes of the sons and daughters of George Drever, Donald Renton and Tom Murray. I see George Murray's daughter, Sheila, impossibly generous with stories and photographs, and William Jackson's girl, Liz, eyes glinting as she recalled her dad drinking with Errol Flynn in Spain.

Their fathers, and those of this book's authors, possessed the kind of foresight and intense convictions typical of those who volunteered to fight in Spain. In the summer of 1936, General Francisco Franco and his reactionary cohort had attempted a military coup that aimed to overthrow Spain's socialistic, democratically elected republican government. The dictatorships of Europe – Hitler's Germany and Mussolini's Italy – sent troops, planes and arms to Franco's Fascist side. Much of Europe turned the other cheek and the Republicans were left to look to the Soviet Union for assistance, and to the tens of thousands of anti-fascist volunteers who travelled from across the world to serve. Most joined the various battalions of the International Brigade, including the British Battalion, those dads among them.

The British Battalion would fight most notably – and often with brutal, heartbreaking consequences – at Jarama, Brunete, Aragon and around the banks of the River Ebro, until the removal of the International Brigades from combat in the autumn of 1938. The following spring, Franco and his allies emerged victorious. Soon, the world was at war, a fate so many Brigaders had foreseen and been engaged in attempting to prevent from happening.

Back home came the living to their streets and their buzzers. Once these 'dirty reds' had overcome the blacklisting and slander of the authorities, most served again and helped bring about fascism's eventual defeat in 1945. And, they returned to their fatherly duties or began new family adventures. None of them were short of stories to tell.

In being told by those who listened to and were affected by those stories, this wonderful and moving book adds something completely original to the Spanish Civil War narrative. It represents, too, the handing on of these vital yarns.

These are individual accounts, full of nuance and difference. Yet they are also representative of fathers (and mothers) from across the world who went to Spain with one shared aim: to smash fascism.

Daniel Gray
October 2022

Introduction

UNTOLD STORIES CONTINUE to emerge about the Scots volunteers who fought in the Spanish Civil War. Compiled in the tradition of collective biography, *Our Fathers Fought Franco* traces the extraordinary journeys of four members of Machine Gun Company No.2 of the British Battalion of the International Brigades. James Maley, Donald Renton, George (Geordie) Watters and Archibald Campbell McAskill (AC) Williams were captured together at the Battle of Jarama in February 1937 and ended up being held together as Prisoners of War in Franco's jails. All too often the characters in accounts of the International Brigades are frozen in time, their lives beyond Spain reduced to a blank page. Instead, this book tells of the hard road these men took to Spain, from their political education and engagement in the 1920s and early 1930s to the risks they faced as volunteers for liberty, and follows these four lives before and after Jarama.

Their story is told in their own words, in the words of family and friends, through newspaper reports, stills cut from newsreels, interviews, letters, diaries, historical accounts, anecdotes and memories. It is illustrated throughout with images and documents, including a unique piece of testimony – the secret notebook kept by AC Williams during his imprisonment.

The poet Pablo Neruda called those who came from all over the world to fight Franco 'the bright ones [...] the victorious fighters [...] that lean, hard, tested rock of a brigade'.[1] On 21 August 1938, a month before he was killed in action at the Ebro, George Green, a member of the International Brigades, wrote home:

Mother dear, we're not militarists, nor adventurers nor professional soldiers: but a few days ago on the hills the other side of the Ebro, I've seen a few unemployed lads from the Clyde, and frightened clerks from Willesden stand up (without fortified positions) against an artillery barrage that professional soldiers could not stand up to. And they did it because to hold the line here and now means that we can prevent this battle being fought again on Hampstead Heath or the hills of Derbyshire.[2]

Green's description of the ordinary men who made up the extraordinary battalions of the International Brigades is almost as poignant as his wife's account of her husband's last moments. According to Nan Green, who was also in Spain nursing the wounded, George, 'killed almost in the last hour of the last day, [...] died flying as it were, you know, like a bird dies'.

In *!Comrades!: Portraits from the Spanish Civil War* (2000), leading historian Paul Preston reminds his readers of the greys between the reds and blacks and blues:

> The conflict was not a tidy split between right and left, between the forces of evil and the forces of good. It was a messy and appallingly painful amalgam of intertwined hostilities and hatreds.[3]

In *Doves of War: Four Women of Spain* (2002), Preston homes in on four 'relatively unknown' female figures from diverse political backgrounds – including Nan Green – to provide a portrait of the war through the eyes of women who experienced it directly. *Our Fathers Fought Franco* also tells the story of relatively unknown participants. All were members of the Communist Party at the time of volunteering, committed antifascists prepared to lay down their lives for the fledgling Spanish Republic. They travelled to Spain at the end of December 1936 – just before the British Government reaffirmed that under the Foreign Enlistment Act it was illegal to recruit or volunteer for service in Spain on either side – and were thrown into battle six weeks later. Their lifelong bond was forged in the crucible of the Battle of Jarama, one of only three episodes in the war where Franco's forces were held at bay, the other two being Madrid from 1936 onwards and Guadalajara in March 1937. But Jarama was a costly defence of the Republic, with half the battalion lost. Many died on the first day.

Before and after Spain, the lives of Maley, Renton, Watters and Williams took different turns, but for a few dark and bloody hours in the Jarama Valley their fates intersected, and for the next few months they spent their days and nights in close proximity as prisoners of Franco. There can of course be no happy ending here; these men fought Franco and Franco won. But in no way did it deflect them from their lifelong commitment to the cause of the Left. Their activism had its roots in the trade union movement, the National Unemployed Workers' Movement (NUWM) and in resistance to the British Union of Fascists (BUF). They were veterans of street fights and strikes, of rallies and speeches. Their hatred of fascism and willingness to take direct action against it was instilled long before they went to Spain. Their lives are emblematic of the grassroots activism and internationalist antifascist action of the times. They were the advance guard in the struggle against fascism.

Spain proved to be a defining moment for the Left, a struggle marked by heroism and sacrifice, but also scarred by sentiment and sectarianism. The communists, anarchists, socialists and republicans from different countries who fought Franco held very different views and at times political differences spilled over into bloodshed. Unlike Germany and Italy, in Spain the fascists won, and Franco stayed in power for nearly 40 years. Why? Partly because the anti-communism that was so central to fascism was shared by many former colonial powers. Churchill hated communism as much as Hitler. But empire is a dimension that is often overlooked. According to Paul Preston, the Spanish Civil War was a colonial war in which

> the right coped with the loss of a 'real' overseas empire by internalising the empire... by regarding metropolitan Spain as the empire and the proletariat as the subject colonial race.[4]

Documenting the experience of these four young working-class men from Glasgow, Portobello, Prestonpans and Portsmouth seems ever more important today, in a world where fascism remains a threat rather than a distant memory.

Willy Maley
October 2022

Notes

1. Pablo Neruda, 'The Arrival in Madrid of the International Brigades', trans. Jodey Bateman, https://motherbird.com/arrival_brigades.html, accessed 18 September 2022. See also Marilyn Rosenthal (ed.), *Poetry of the Spanish Civil War* (New York: New York University Press, 1975), 297.
2. Cited in Paul Preston, *Doves of War: Four Women of Spain* (London: HarperCollins, 2002), 170–71.
3. Paul Preston, *!Comrades!: Portraits from the Spanish Civil War* (Glasgow: Fontana Press, 2000), 8.
4. Paul Preston, 'The Answer Lies in the Sewers: Captain Aguilera and the Mentality of the Francoist Officer Corps', *Science & Society* 68, 3 (2004): 277–312, at 281.

Timeline

1931

14 April	Second Spanish Republic proclaimed.

1936

16 February	In Spain the Popular Front wins elections.
10 May	Manuel Azaña becomes President.
17 July	A military uprising in Spanish Morocco is followed next day by a rising in Spain, signalling the start of Civil War, with Franco leading the Army of Africa.
4 August	Anglo-French Non-Intervention Treaty signed.
4 September	Popular Front government formed with Republicans, Socialists and Communists.
	Four anarchist ministers join the Popular Front government
23	October Rome–Berlin Axis signed.
8 November	Arrival of International Brigades in Madrid.
	The battle begins for control of Madrid, with Franco aiming to effect a siege.
27 December	The Saklatvala Battalion – later the British Battalion – comes into being.

1937

11 January	British Government confirms that under the Foreign Enlistment Act it is illegal to recruit or volunteer for service in Spain on either side.
6 February	Battle of Jarama begins.
8 February	Málaga falls to Franco's forces.
9 March	Franco issues an order that all foreigners captured with arms will be executed.
26 April	The Luftwaffe bomb Guernica, the heart of the Basque region.
3–9 May	Republicans and Communists suppress an anarchist and Trotskyist rising in Barcelona.
19 June	Franco takes Bilbao.
6 July	Republican counter-offensive at Brunete.

23 August	Republican counter-offensive at Belchite fails to stem fascist advance.
13 October	Battle of Ebro begins.
17 December	British Battalion in action as Republicans take Teruel.

1938

8 January	Teruel recaptured by Franco's forces.
25 July	A Republican counter-offensive across the River Ebro proves unsuccessful.
1 August	The 15th Brigade launch attack on Hill 481 near Gandesa.
22 September	Last action of British Battalion. Juan Negrín, leader of the Republican government, announces withdrawal of the International Brigades.
30 September	Munich Agreement signed by Britain, France, Germany and Italy.
28 October	International Brigades honoured with a farewell parade through Barcelona and speech by Isadora Dolores Ibárruri Gómez, 'La Pasionaria'.
23 December	Franco attacks Catalonia.

1939

26 January	Fall of Barcelona.
27 February	British Government recognises Franco as the legitimate authority in Spain.
28 March	Franco's forces enter Madrid.
1 April	Spanish Civil War ends.
1 September	Germany invades Poland, triggering the outbreak of WW2.

I

JAMES MALEY
'Neath the Red Flag I would fight

Willy Maley

MY FATHER, JAMES MALEY, died aged 99 on 9 April 2007. On seeing his obituary, a military historian contacted the family and asked if he could have access to his papers before they were deposited in a library. He was surprised to learn that the only physical records of his time in Spain were two photographs, frames taken from a 1937 newsreel. My father rarely wrote anything down and when he died his papers consisted only of a passport from January 1930 when he emigrated to the USA. But in a way he left something of more lasting value than documents: on 12 July 2004, three years before his death, he gave a filmed interview to Craig Curran. At 96 years of age, he was still as sharp as a tack. It wasn't until 2015 that Craig converted the film to digital format and it was posted on YouTube. Dini Power transcribed the audio that same year, so there is now a written record. In 2019 another interview surfaced, audio only, one that my father had given to the Imperial War Museum (IWM) on Tuesday 9 April 1991, when he was a youthful 83 years old. This was part of an emerging archive. It was fascinating for his family to hear their father's voice from this time talking animatedly about Spain to Conrad Wood who, like Craig Curran, was an excellent interviewer, and managed to catch him at a time when he had more anecdotes on the tip of his tongue than in Craig's film.

Wood's interview was part of a series. By the early 1980s the IWM had completed an initial project on Spain: 'Thirty-five interviews with British volunteers who fought with the International Brigade and with informants who served in other capacities during the Spanish Civil War'. My father was a late addition. Most of the interview with Conrad Wood – two of the three reels, each running for half an hour, are about the Spanish Civil War; in the third reel, the shortest section at about 15 minutes, he talks about his time in India and Burma during the Second World War. The Spanish side of his wartime experiences had been quite well covered, his time in India and Burma less so.

In these interviews, with very few exceptions, my father never names his comrades. As he says himself, 'I never bothered much about names.' The fact that MI5 was keeping tabs on him – the Communist Party was vulnerable to infiltration and its members were subject to surveillance – would have been a factor. Something else that strikes you about his recollection of his time as a prisoner of Franco in 1937 is that he never complains about mistreatment. He recalls how he saw a man having his brains blown out right in front of him and being punched in the face himself. He was stuck in a cell with nine men, infested with lice. There was a dry toilet with no paper and very little to eat or drink, and they would see the 'death van' appear at the place where they were being held. Yet he says he was 'never ill-treated once'. That's just the way he was, the same James Maley who would drink from the Irrawaddy River a few years later while dead bodies floated past. Recalling his time as a POW in Spain, he talks of being pulled up for singing republican songs, laughs about the capitan with the green hair, and recounts an interrogation in which he had to prove his Catholic faith by reciting 'one or two of the Hail Maleys'. That slip of the tongue stood out in the original audiotape.

My father always spoke quickly, like a machine gun, so the transcriptions took time. It was decided that the reel covering his years in India and Burma, would be transcribed first. Some words were impossible to make out, no matter how many times the reel was replayed, but most of what he said was captured. The IWM interview was conducted a few months after the first performance of the play *From the Calton to Catalonia*, written by my brother John and myself, based loosely on our father's time in Spain and taking the two frames from the lost newsreel as a starting-point. The strange thing is, we never thought to interview our father. We'd heard some of his stories but knew very little about his time in Spain beyond the fact of his being there, his capture and the images cut from the newsreel.

When writing the play, we drew on printed sources like David Corkill and Stuart Rawnsley's *The Road to Spain: Anti-fascists at War 1936–1939* (1981) and Iain MacDougall's *Voices from the Spanish Civil War: Personal Recollections of Scottish Volunteers in Republican Spain, 1936–39* (1986). James's voice wasn't among the International Brigade members interviewed for those collections of first-hand accounts by members of the International Brigades. In fact, it was the absence of his voice from oral histories like these that spurred us into writing the play. My father had shown a lifetime of commitment but was rarely recognised, except locally. He had a habit of falling out with people and maybe this is why he never seemed to be included in rolls of honour.

There was another reason why interviewing my father about the past was difficult: his mind was nearly always focused on the present and the future. It was not that he never looked back, just that he was always watching the news and reading the papers, including *The Beijing Review* and *The Soviet Weekly*. Journalists who wanted to speak to him about Spain had to persist in order to get past Iraq, Afghanistan, and in the end, Sudan. But by doggedly getting James to stick to the subject, Conrad Wood and Craig Curran teased out some great vignettes.

Oral history is a unique way to capture the memories of those who don't leave behind a written record. It is a crucial means of preserving working-class history, so-called 'history from below'. The Spanish Civil War has been discussed at length by writers and historians but the voices of volunteers are vital in painting a fuller picture of what happened. In what follows, the aim is to let my father's voice tell as much of the story as possible. In the absence of letters and diaries these interviews are his testament.

James Maley was imprisoned twice in his life. In 1985 he spent two nights in the cells after being arrested under the Prevention of Terrorism Act for selling a paper called *Ireland's War*. On Monday 26 August that year he appeared at Hamilton Sheriff Court accused of committing a breach of the peace in Carfin, Lanarkshire the previous Saturday by

> repeatedly thrusting documents entitled Ireland's War at the public and attempting to sell them to their alarm and annoyance, or alternatively a contravention of section 21B of the Prevention of Terrorism Act alleging he carried or displayed such documents to arouse reasonable suspicion that he was a member or supporter of the IRA.

Charged with an offence under the PTA, he was released on bail pending trial, set for 17 February 1986, but the absurdity of the accusation and the intervention of several MPs, across parties, including Labour's Joan Maynard, led to all charges being dropped on 14 November 1985. Remember that this happened not in Franco's Spain, where censorship was rife, but in a country where the title of a Linda and Paul McCartney song – 'Give Ireland Back to the Irish' (1972) – couldn't even be read out on the BBC, yet managed to reach No.1 in Ireland and, ironically, in Spain. A few weeks after his arrest, on Saturday 5 October 1985, James Maley stood to attention at the unveiling of the memorial to the International Brigades at the Jubilee Gardens in London, arm-in-arm with his closest comrade-in-arms, his wife Anne. My father was known in his younger days and among his Communist Party comrades to the end as 'Jimmy'. James is used here – his Sunday name – because that was what my mother called him, and she always had the last word.

Early Life

The fifth of nine children, James Maley was born at 9am on Wednesday 19 February 1908 at 47 Kirk Street in the Calton district of Glasgow, in the heart of the city's East End. The street name later changed to Stevenson Street, where the family address was No. 136. His parents were a familiar mix of Irish and Scottish. 'Scots steel tempered wi' Irish fire / Is the weapon that I desire', wrote Hugh MacDiarmid in 'The Weapon' (1930), and James certainly had that fusion. His father, Edward Maley, known as Ned, was born in Rossanrubble, Newport, Co. Mayo on Monday 10 July 1871, the same day as Marcel Proust, and just six weeks after the bloody suppression of the Paris Commune.

There is no surviving photograph of Ned, but James remembered his father as a short man with a 50-inch chest. Ned worked as a corporation navvy – or causewayers' labourer – on the roads. James's mother, Anne Sherlock, was born at 24 Adelphi Street in the Gorbals, Glasgow, on Saturday 24 May 1879. She was a hawker and James worked from an early age helping his mother wheel her barrow around Glasgow. Sometimes he'd take the empty barrow home with his wee brothers sitting in it. Anne and Ned married in Glasgow on Friday 8 July 1898, their trades stated respectively as 'fabric spinner' and 'mason's labourer'.

Of their nine children, only five survived into adulthood. Infant mortality was high among Glasgow's East End poor and four of James's brothers never made it past the age of ten – three never made it to a year. John, born on 24 January 1899, died of bronchitis aged two weeks. Michael, born on 24 November 1899 died of bronchopneumonia at four months. Perhaps the saddest story is that of the two Edwards. The first Edward, born on 12 January 1901, died on 20 March 1911. This is an older brother that James remembered well, always running, a choirboy, who developed breathing problems. The death certificate says 'Valvular disease of the Heart 3 months Pneumonia 8 days'. His parents tried again, giving their next son the same name. Born on 28 April 1912, he died of bronchopneumonia on 2 December 1912. James remembered the keening and the cuddles. Between times, three other children were born: Annie (31.7.1903), William (2.2.1910), and Timothy (24.11.1913). The last of Anne Sherlock's children, Mary, was born on 5 February 1917. Interestingly, the birth certificate for Mary has under Surname 'Sherlock or Maley' and notes that her mother is 'Annie Sherlock, Hawker, wife of Edward Maley, Labourer, who she declares is not the father of the child'.

James's parents separated at the time of Mary's birth, and he recalled going round to his mother's house to see his wee sister, Mary. His father was away from home for a time too, and James recalls turning a woman away from the door who came with a pot of soup, which he took as nosiness disguised as charity. He'd have been about nine years old at the time. Educated at St Alphonsus in Greendyke Street, he remembered the Calton as a particularly unruly and unlawful neighbourhood:

> Oh, aye, it was a hard area. It was a rowdy area, so far as the police were concerned. They hated – I must say this – they hated the police. The police were the enemy [...] Oh there were fights every Saturday night, last for hours.

James was radicalised from an early age. Politics was in the air he breathed. He recalls when he was five seeing a short film entitled *The Yellow Peril*. This film, made in 1908, is notorious for its anti-Chinese and anti-Irish stereotypes. He knew which side he should take – always the underdog. The following year, James watched the soldiers marching to the railway station in Glasgow, and soon heard about battleships, including the Clyde-built HMS *Inflexible*, being involved in the Battle of the Falklands on 8 December 1914.

In the 1991 IWM interview with Conrad Wood, James reflected on his early schooling and mentions hearing about Jack London, even before he knew who that author was:

> I got to realise that religion was the opium of the people, and that the Labour Party were also the enemy of the people. And when the young men came home from the First World War I heard them talking at the street corners about *The Iron Heel*. Although I didn't know too much about what *The Iron Heel* was about I was interested in listening to them. And there was also a paper called *John Bull* that was fighting on behalf of the ex-soldiers after the First World War, and times were bad then. There were no jobs for the ones who came home from the First World War. Some of these men who came home in 1918 never worked except for two jobs from the dole, from the labour exchange.

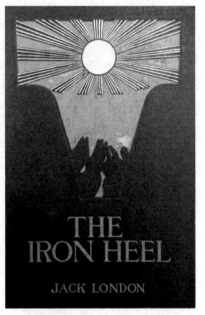

As a boy, James Maley heard 'street corner' talk of Jack London's novel about a fascist takeover of the United States.

One of the jobs the returning soldiers got was working at Palacerigg Labour Colony in South Cumbernauld, run by the Glasgow Distress Committee, producing peat. A fire-lighter factory opened there in 1923. This was no land fit for heroes. James recalled street corner conversations about the causes of the war and the false promises given to soldiers and their families. This was Red Clydeside, the Calton a seedbed of socialism. Out on an errand on 31 January 1919, James took a detour to George Square, where he witnessed the events of 'Bloody Friday', when 20,000 protesters were attacked by police and the Red Flag was raised.

James left school at 14 and started work selling rolls and cakes round the doors. He used to go to political meetings and report back on who was worth listening to. At Glasgow Green he heard James Maxton, leader of the

Independent Labour Party (ILP), among others. In 1926, during the General Strike, James contracted pneumonia and was hospitalised. Considered to be at death's door, he was given the last rites by a priest summoned to his bedside. James remembered hearing the sound of a band in the distance.

Whether it was the priest or the rousing sound of the pipes that did it, James was soon back on his feet. But the harsh times for the family continued. The following year James's Uncle Michael, Ned's younger brother, was hit by a tram and died of his injuries. Then three years after his near-death experience, James had to bury his own father: Edward 'Ned' Maley died of pulmonary tuberculosis in Stobhill Hospital on Sunday 17 November 1929. All the Irish relatives came over for Ned's funeral and were taken aback by the poverty of the Glasgow branch.

James emigrated to the United States in January 1930. This process was set in motion by the death of his father, and also that of his uncle, triggering a series of letters from his Irish aunts, Anne and Mary, in Cleveland, Ohio. They considered James as the vanguard of a fresh wave of emigration, 30 or 40 years after they themselves had settled in America, married, and had children there. James's Uncle John also wrote from Rossanrubble on 7 January 1930 encouraging emigration for James's cousins, Uncle Michael's orphaned children. James sailed to New York aboard the *President Harding* on New Year's Day 1930, arriving at Ellis Island on 9 January. Under 'Employment' his passenger record says 'cabinet maker'. For those of us who remember his handiwork, that raises an eyebrow and a smile but you probably had to say you had a skill. One of James's Irish relatives in Cleveland, his Aunt Anne, had written on his father's death: 'I was glad to hear your Father had the Priest. Poor Michael he had no chance to have a Priest.' Both aunts, though welcoming, cautioned against misconceptions of easy opportunities in America. These were hard times for new immigrants.

James got a job in a candy factory in Cleveland, an hour's streetcar journey from Lakewood, where he lived with his Aunt Mary, then found work at the White Motor Car Company on Canal Street. At the car plant James got into an argument with some co-workers, but when a crowd of them came running down the metal stairs at the end of the shift to see James waiting for them, alone and unafraid, they let it drop. Another story he told was that once he went to a ten-cents-a-dance event, saw a woman who wasn't being danced, walked over to her, gave her all his tickets and left. Despite the fact that his aunts were well settled in the States, James was restless and homesick

James Maley aged 22 at his aunt's house in
Cleveland Ohio, 1930.

James Maley in his Sunday best, Ohio, 1930.
Not his car – he never learned to drive.

and he returned to Glasgow in September 1931, tanned and smartly dressed, carrying a case. His brother, thinking he was selling something, closed the door on him.

James and his comrades came to political maturity in the 1920s and '30s, experiencing the Hunger Marches, the Depression and the rise of fascism. They were a distinctive generation: self-taught, autodidacts, working-class activists and agitators with no or few formal qualifications, but very well-read. Back in Glasgow, James began to take part in political demonstrations. He had in the 1920s been quite sympathetic to the Independent Labour Party, which had a strong Glasgow base, but he joined the Parkhead branch of the Communist Party on 16 February 1932, just before his 24th birthday, quickly becoming an active member. As he recalled, 'two weeks later I was on the platform, speaking'. He was a nominee for the May Day delegation to the USSR but did not go. His focus was on local activism, and he became a regular and well-known speaker, carrying his collapsible platform from Glasgow Green to Govan Cross, or wherever there were meetings. One of his soapbox stops, one of many speakers' corners dotted around the city, was at the junction of Rose Street and Sauchiehall Street. When he was walking along Argyle Street, tram drivers tooted their horns, recognising him as a speaker and comrade.

Yet James never held any formal position in the Party. According to his MI5 file dating from this period, James was '5ft 6inches, slim build, dark brown hair, tanned complexion, grey eyes'.

He never sought office of any kind. He took an avid interest in world affairs and watched events unfold in Spain with the rise of Hitler in Germany and the miners' strike in the Asturias in October 1934, seen as a prelude to the events of July 1936.

Well, in 1934 I found out there was trouble in Spain up in the Asturias. They were fighting for their sort of independence. [...] I read it through papers. And I decided there and then that I was going to join the Territorials and get some army experience. And I joined the 58th Cameronians [in] West Princes Street in 1934. When I went there to join up there were 17 people there actually passed the doctor [...] Well after you passed the doctor you were to go up and see the man above, the heid man at the time, and only two actually got into the Territorials. A young boy of 17 and myself were the only two that got accepted. The other 15 weren't, although they had passed the doctor. That was the 58th Cameronians, they must have been very particular. And I went, we were in Girvan the first year, putting up the tents, and then to Cambuslang for the shooting [...]. So I learned how to shoot, bullseye, bullseye. And I knew then, when the war came in '36, I wasnae going there as somebody that had to learn anything, and I knew what to do, that's the main thing.

In the Territorial Army James learned how to use a rifle on the ranges at Dechmont Camp, Cambuslang. He reflected on the fact that other International Brigaders never had this training: 'I knew I was able to shoot. And I knew how to look after myself. While some of them who went on these buses had never seen a rifle, except in the pictures.' Asked why he joined the International Brigades in 1936 James replied:

Well you see, being in the Communist Party and being a speaker I'd been speaking about Hitler from the time he took power in 1933, January. So I was, I was like a teacher in school, I learned things by heart all the time, every move that was made, the British

Anglo-German naval agreement, the march into the Rhineland and all these things, and then Austria and the Sudetenland and then the Munich agreement [...] so I knew what I was talking about.

James went on to explain that he felt he had to go to prove that he was more than just a speaker:

Well you see, there was no good of me speaking of the menace of fascism and all this sort of thing, and not going to fight about it myself. But I mean I wouldn't ask anybody else to do something that I wasn't going to do myself. So I volunteered and went [...] You see well the position I was in, I was staying in Shettleston although I was in the Parkhead branch, and the MP for Shettleston had went to Spain and came back and made a big attack on the Catholic Church. So it didn't go down too well with a lot of people in Shettleston, so he went back the second time and then he came back and made a big attack on the Communist Party, but he didn't retract what he had said about the Catholic Church, and by a bit of bad luck for one of the three councillors, who was himself a Catholic, Councillor Heenan, he was standing at that time for the council, and they were held at that time on the first Tuesday of November, and for the first time in Shettleston the ILP candidate got beat because of the campaign against him. And he had never mentioned Spain. And it was after that that I went to Spain.

Many working-class Catholics defied the church to fight for the Spanish Republic. International Brigaders from Ireland and Scots from Irish-Catholic backgrounds fought for the British Battalion of the xvth International Brigade. Like other comrades from Glasgow, James was a Catholic who didn't heed the advice of the church hierarchy – which was to support Franco. In fact, Steve Fullarton, a fellow International Brigader, said James liked to goad the young Catholic men in the audience who had come fresh from their dose of pulpit propaganda. A lot of Scots were on the soapbox in the 1930s, with Catholic denunciations of communism going hand-in-hand with Irish Republican and socialist denunciations of the church's stance. The East End of Glasgow was a particular crucible of contention, drawing as it did great support for communists, anarchists and ILP-ers.

John McGovern, Independent Labour Party MP for Shettleston, went to Spain in November 1936 and wrote a pamphlet called *Why Bishops Back Franco*, based on a speech he gave at Glasgow City Hall on Sunday 13 December 1936. McGovern angered his Catholic constituents by railing against the Church in Spain in what Tom Gallagher called 'perhaps the most anti-clerical speech ever given by a Glasgow Labour MP'. As a Catholic radical McGovern took issue with right-wing Catholics. McGovern also angered his communist opponents in 1937 with his pamphlet on the 'Red Terror', and much later angered almost everyone when he recommended backing the Tories. James hated anti-Catholic prejudice, but he hated fascist Catholics even more. Spain was a deeply divisive issue. The Ancient Order of Hibernians

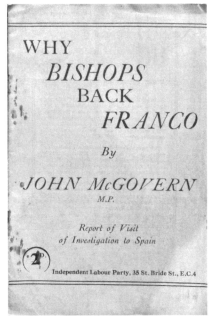

The Independent Labour Party MP for Shettleston John McGovern railed against the support given to Franco by the Catholic clergy.

had come out against the Spanish Republic and in support of the fascists in August 1936. The Catholic Union of Scotland was loudly pro-Franco. Willie Gallacher, Communist MP for West Fife, was heckled at meetings in his constituency by Catholic supporters of Franco. James described his decision to go to Spain in a characteristically matter-of-fact way:

> I was a labourer, just a general labourer, and when the Spanish thing came up, I recognised right from wrong. This was the first time there had been an attempt made by working-class people to take power and they were being attacked. And I was a member of the Communist Party, and I volunteered along with the rest to go to Spain.

On Thursday 31 December 1936, James left from George Square in Glasgow on one of three double-decker buses bound for London, buses so packed there were men standing. He was just one of many with revolutionary, Irish and republican interests and commitments who emerged from the slums of Glasgow and Edinburgh, and from the shipyards, coalfields and factories of Scotland. All the arrangements were made by the Communist Party. At the time he was living with his widowed mother at 500 Old Shettleston Road, and he saw men there from neighbouring closes. On the bus from Glasgow were several men James recognised from Celtic matches:

Well they all came [...] mainly from the East End of Glasgow. And as I say, I knew quite a lot of them, they'd been on hunger marches and I'd been on the marches so I knew who they were. And it all seemed to be one of them cases, 99 per cent were Catholics. And Spain was a Catholic country. So it proved the old, old saying that in all religions there's the rich and the poor and that's it.

James's views on religion were complicated. Raised a Catholic, he experienced anti-Catholic bigotry – which in Scotland was bound up with anti-Irish prejudice – and later he was on the receiving-end of anti-Communist sentiment that affected his employment opportunities. Asked about his decision to go to Spain when the Catholic Church backed Franco, James responded:

I wasn't opposed to the Catholic Church, well I mean I never mentioned religion, if people want to go, go, but [...] see, when I was at school I realised that – I was asked to become a priest a lot of times at school but I realised to become a priest, well it wasn't an easy job to become or do, I mean if you believed in religion then it was something you'd have to... be different from other people. I mean you'd have to be, live different from the ordinary person, whereas at the present time if I stood at the corner, I realised if I stood at the corner and watched people passing by, even where I lived I couldn't say that's a Catholic, that's a Protestant. I mean there was nothing to define them, they all just lived the same. But to be a priest you'd have to live different. And that's something, well, I wasn't prepared to do.

James explained how he came to be the first member of the Communist Party to join up from his branch:

See, although I was in the Parkhead branch I stayed in Shettleston
[…] well, what happened was this, was that although I was in the
Parkhead branch in 1935, February, I moved to Shettleston […]
I started a Shettleston branch, and started speaking in Shettleston,
and for that year and a half before I went to Spain […] I began to
realise and after I went another half a dozen or so went.

James's route to Spain was straightforward. From London, the
volunteers travelled to Dunkirk on Sunday 3 January 1937:

Just went quite simple, went to London. I went to the pictures that
night, then we got the boat train to Paris and stopped in Paris, and
then went through to Spain.

In Paris, they stopped off at Communist Party Headquarters in Place du
Combat, a hub for the movement of volunteers, and went from there by
rail down through Perpignan and Figueres to Albacete, where they were
issued with uniforms, then on to Madrigueras for training.
James recalled:

It was like a Czech uniform, you know, the khaki, but the trousers
had the elastic here and they just folded over the boots, like, like
everything else we got rigged out.

James was issued with a Russian rifle that was new and easy for him to
handle: 'So I could fire the gun, know what I mean. Some people are just
natural at firing the rifle.'
Asked why he had joined the Territorials James replied: 'Well, you see,
as they say, coming events cast their shadow before, and I knew the war
was coming.'
James habitually walked 20 or 30 miles a day and was in great physical
condition. Asked if he was a good shot he responded:

Well I'll tell you a funny thing about being a good shot. I was a
half-decent shot, but I always knew that I could kill the other man.
It's not, see, I knew what the other person was gonnae do. That's
the main thing.

He was good at reading people's expressions and had a knack for interpreting meaning despite not sharing a common language. While in Madrigueras, for example, James took food to a local family after an encounter with a hungry child:

> Well [...] the first day I was there a little boy spoke to me. I didn't
> know what he was talking about but I knew what he meant and
> I got some food and went with him and took it to his mother.[...]
> I got them some army tinned stuff, you know.

After five weeks' training at Madrigueras, James was in action at the Battle of Jarama in February 1937 as part of a heavy-machine gun company, covering the retreat for three days. James recalled literally jumping out of the back of a lorry into a battlefield. He described it later as like coming out of a close into a street fight. When the time came to move it all happened very quickly, with Machine Gun Company No. 2 being moved to the front line in lorries with eight Russian-made Maxim machine guns: 'The ones on wheels. [...] Pre-war, you know, 1914.' James was part of No. 2 Machine Gun Company, one of four companies in the British Battalion. The Company spent what little time they had learning how to operate the Russian water-cooled Maxim machine-guns.

The Company was commanded by Harold Fry and Ted Dickenson. What happened next was carnage. James described the sudden drama of the move to the Jarama front on Friday 12 February 1937:

> Everybody outside all at once, all lined up [...] and we were put
> in different squads. I was put into the machine gun squad, and
> that was like we had two guns each squad, two men to a gun,
> that was 60 men and [...] we had 12 men with us who were just
> for the rifles, a support group, and that was off to battle, Jarama.
> [...] And all of a sudden we found ourselves in the war. [...] 'Out,
> everybody out!', and the drivers turned round and away with the
> motors again, the lorries. And we were in the war, and it was hell
> of a ... it was some bloody war.

That Friday night, 12 February, there was an eerie silence. The men were afraid to speak in case they give away their position:

We were there that night and you hear voices and you don't know whether it's wounded or not. We didn't know if it was real or not or if it was a decoy because the Spaniards knew English and we could hear 'Help, help' all the Friday night but what could we do? We couldn't do much about it. And that was it [...] Oh aye, well I was wondering what they were doing at home, or what I'd have been doing at home, especially when it came to the Saturday morning, daylight, well that's when we got our first shell fired at us. [...] you'd nothing else to think about except if you wanted to do the toilet you had to go to the back of a tree and while you were doing it, whatever you were going to do, there was whssht of the bullets.

The Battle of Jarama was one of the costliest encounters of the war, particularly for the International Brigades. The company engaged in heavy fighting over the weekend of 12 and 13 February 1937. Half the 500-strong British Battalion were killed or wounded. Only 125 of the 400 members of the rifle companies survived. It was particularly costly for No. 2 Machine Gun Company. As one comrade, Tommy Bloomfield, later recalled: 'Of our 120 men, three had gone back for ammo, we had 29 survivors, and the rest were killed.' Those 29 survivors were captured on 13 February while covering the retreat on 'Suicide Hill'. James described the scene:

There were soldiers running past us and we were going up. Actually there was soldiers out of the British Battalion dropping, going up, without firing a shot, getting killed [...] And some of our chaps actually going through got killed without having seen the enemy.

James knew of only one man who had fought before, in the First World War. The rest were raw recruits. His own Territorial Army training hadn't prepared him for this kind of pitched battle:

We saw them dying before our eyes... They were retreating all the time, and all of a sudden we were left, and over on that right hand side was the Franco-Belgians and they were retreating too and we just emptied the machine guns [...] until there were no bullets left, [...] and they were all away behind us in the battle. No more did we hear the sounds of the war or nothing, but that was us left there. We couldnae go back, couldnae go anywhere. And that was a Friday night.

The war in Spain was different from the First World War. It was fought on the barricades as well as the battlefield, on streets and among olive groves, on university campuses and civic squares. James remembered the scene at Jarama:

> There were no trenches. When we went they were retreating, we weren't in a trench. They were retreating, it was a slow process. It was a wide, wide area, about twice the size of a football field, more than that. And coming down the right-hand side were the Spaniards. And our crowd of course got off the lorries and joined them. So there was a mass, a mass of fucking hell, and we were firing the machine guns. Well, we know them at the back's the enemy. And then gradually they disappeared out of sight. The Franco-Belgians were on the other side coming down from that end and we fired the guns, then when they got to here our friends are at the front, the enemy's at the back chasing them down, and we just blazed away with the machine guns till the bullets were done. That's all we could do. That's the only thing about us. You see you've got to have ammunition coming up for the guns. The bullets don't last forever.

While the bullets lasted Machine Gun Company No. 2 played its part in holding the line:

> Well, we could hear the firing on both sides of us, but the only ones we ever saw were the Franco-Belgians on our right. They'd be about 150 yards further on, on our right, a good distance away, but [...] we could see them plain enough, and we seen them getting up, falling back, down, up, falling back, slowly retreating. So we turned our machine guns on an angle right across in front of them. So firing at that range, in order for to slow down the ones who were chasing them, though we couldn't get a right view of them. Just a crossfire. But everything after that on the first day was an awful lull, as if there was nobody in the place. And we were there and we wondered what was up but we stuck there where we were.

The second day had a strange stillness about it: 'On Saturday morning we got our first shell, one shell. Two hours passed, and we got another shell.' The men were stuck in limbo awaiting ammunition and orders:

We stayed there and then we started to get shells down again. But the first morning, the next morning, they came up with food, some of them. It was big bowls like apple jelly and, like ham and that, and they told us that they were trying to form a line further back. So we stayed where we were. And it would be like a pantomime. We never actually saw all the day on the Saturday another soldier. Everything deathly quiet, until Sunday we got up now and again to go further back behind some of the olive groves.

The olive groves were a flimsy defence, but they offered some cover, and they also served as a latrine. A diet of olives made that an essential factor:

And then we could hear the firing. And I went myself, but you're sitting down and under a tree and the leaves were falling on top of me because they were starting to shoot then. [...] If anybody went to the toilet they would see them then and they would start to fire. Rifle fire. And the leaves were falling down on top of me, but you were just doing it and crawling back into the little trench we had dug. But then the shelling started after that. But we stuck where we were because we knew we had a good field of fire, but what we didn't know was that they were coming on both sides of us, they were coming through [...] Well we were outflanked. We could have removed but with staying where we were in a way we held up the through advance in front of us.

James found grim humour in some of the scenes, but he also expressed deep sadness and regret:

I'm only sorry to say that a lot of good men died. In one day. The battalion never was the same. And after that it was whenever two Britishers come over to Spain they were put in among the Spaniards, another two or three would come, they were put in among the Spaniards, but the British battalion was finished, that one day.

35

James described the moment of capture in stark terms: 'Then gradually the Moors appeared mounted on horses and we were surrounded and rounded up.' What happened next began with threats and ended in death:

> They had come through the flanks on each side. We were only 28 men in a wee group, and as I said, the olive groves was a big, huge place. Everybody had moved back. [...] Well the Spanish ... the Moors were making gestures with... they had these wee sort of sabres, wee sort of curved, that they were going to cut the privates off us. Aye. [laughs] And eh... I didn't know what this one said to me but he punched me right in the face, aye he punched me right in the face. [...] I think it was because I didn't understand what he was telling me to do.

When the machine gun company was captured and lined up, Ted Dickenson was pulled out first and James recalled vividly the actions that ensued:

> The two Spanish soldiers on the other side stepped forward and, eh, blew his brains out. [...] Oh aye, it was like somebody just doing that. With somebody's forehead, just doing that and opening it. Aye. Eh... somebody spoke and I heard a voice saying, 'Don't shoot, they're English.' They thought we were Russians. With the uniforms. At first. And eh, Fry, only for that Fry would have been shot too, we would all have been shot one at a time. Aye, somebody shouted 'English'. They heard us. Aye. English. Ingleses. In the line. Or else we'd all have been shot.

James later reflected: 'I think we were lucky in the sense that any other group being captured that wasn't English, British, would have had a rougher time. I think that's what saved us, that we happened just to be British'.

Phil Ellis from Leeds was shot when he reached into his pocket for a cigarette (which he had asked to do and had the okay). Ted Dickenson, second-in-command, was shot because he was recognised as an officer. That left 27 men, who had their thumbs tied with telephone wire and were forced along on foot behind enemy lines by Moorish cavalry:

> We were taken to a place called Talavera de la Reina. [...] Well we were nine to a cell. And eh, it was one big dish of food. And we

all ate out of it with our hands. And there was a wee toilet in the corner that you couldn't flush. And you couldn't wash your hands. And there was no toilet paper. And the nine of us ate with our hands out of that dish all the time it came in. There was nothing to drink, it was a thick, a sort of mass of whatever it was, but we all ate off our hands. Hands were... which proves you can do a lot of things when you're hungry.

James was older than most of his comrades. He turned 29 on 19 February, in a Spanish jail. He was ten years older than some of the young men he saw die, including the Spaniards who were executed in the prison. Conditions were harsh, but James accepted that this was the cost of capture and never wavered in his conviction that going to Spain was the right thing to do. James had lived and worked under difficult circumstances all his life, but even for someone with a strong stomach there was a limit to how far he would go to eat:

And still the [...] same thing for eating, they came in with [...] like a basin full of soup, and we ate off that, we were dished out of that into a plate and we got a round thing again, with the bread. That was to do you for the day. Except for one day, by a bit of luck I was in the front. But this big Irishman was in the middle and when it was his turn he leaned over it and his bread fell into the soup and he took off the army jacket and rolled up the sleeves and his hand was down feeling for the loaf, and all the ones at the back of him got off their mark, by Christ. Who was going to eat after that, except him? And that soup was taken away, what was left of it, and the following day it was just filled up and taken back in again and that was our grub.

After two weeks at Talavera de la Reina the men were moved on again:

We got interrogated when we went to the next place. The next place [...] It was a big barn. And in this there would be about a hundred men. Most of them were young Spaniards. And then there was our 27. There were two Germans. Dos Alemanes. And one Frenchman. And one Britisher who we didn't know was British at the start, who had come off … he'd been on a ship, a merchant ship. And he'd got off at Spain and he was shouting to hell… he was saying to hell with Franco. [Laughs] And he was there too.

One thing James did complain about was the lice, which were rife and hard to shift:

Lice was the only thing we had in the barn. […] You'd lie down, ye see we had wur uniform. The only thing we had on was still wur uniform, all the time, we never had them off. And this barn, down each side of the barn and along the top was boards that came out to about five feet, boards out from here to there, right up the sides, round the back, and down the other side. Well we lay on that wi our legs, feet, half off it. Well ye'd waken up through the night wi somebody standing above ye. Lying next to you. And you just felt up the legs of your trousers, and your trousers off, hundreds a lice.

He was later interrogated by Pablo Merry Del Val, Chief Liaison Officer for the foreign press under Franco. James told of how the religion he declared himself to be was significant: 'That was one of the questions. […] What religion we were. […] I just said Catholic. I'm a Catholic.' Asked to say a couple of Hail Marys James obliged and that seemed to satisfy his interrogator.

The Merry del Vals were a fascinating family. The man who interrogated James was one of the sons of Alfonso Merry Del Val, the former Spanish ambassador to Britain. Pablo Merry Del Val, educated at Stonyhurst College, a Jesuit boarding school in Clitheroe, Lancashire, was part of a prominent family of clerics and diplomats of Irish descent – 'Wild Geese' from Waterford. His brother Alfonso was the author of a pamphlet entitled *The Conflict in Spain: Communistic Misstatements Refuted*, published in London by the Catholic Truth Society in 1937, and was Franco's unofficial representative in England at the time. The family had fingers in many pies and this may have been the same Dr Pablo Merry del Val, later the Cultural Relations Consul of the Spanish Embassy in Washington, selling Franco to the Americans after the war, and afterwards Spanish ambassador to the US.

James talked a lot all his life, but he knew when to act daft and how not to answer questions. He could spot a state agent at a hundred yards:

They asked me about this and that. You know, regarding the war and that, you see, but after he'd listened to me speaking I heard him say to the other ones who were there: he knows F.A. He knows nothing. You see I gave him... see, you can know a lot of things and you can know nothing about the war, but you could be tortured for something you don't know. Whereas I can give the impression that I don't know.

During interrogations, Bert 'Yank' Levy, who was actually a Canadian – Isaac Meyer Levy (1897–1965), who would go on to write a book called *Guerrilla Warfare* (1941) – advised the men to answer truthfully but slyly. Why were they in Spain? To do a job of work. When would they leave? When the job was done. Things improved. The first day the prisoners got 'one ration and two bashings'. The second day they got 'two rations and one bashing'. The bashings came from Germans and Moors. Harold Fry and Jimmy Rutherford were sentenced to death, the others to 20 years.

Harold Fry. Drawing c. 1937, reproduced in *Records of the 15th Brigade* published by the Commissariat of War, XV Brigade, Madrid 1938

Although he stood up to the harsh conditions and rough treatment, James recalled another occasion when he thought his number was up:

Well, we got a fright one time. The big van, there was a sort of death van. And it came this time and eh, we were all up and we were talking about making a go for it out the door, going to the door and saying 'latrete' [?], and when the guard opened the door, when he was outside the door, we were going to make one rush. [Laughs]. But eh, it passed by.

While they were in prison, a curious thing happened. A propaganda newsreel made on Tuesday 23 March 1937 showing the prisoners being handed cigarettes in the courtyard was screened in a cinema in Glasgow. James's mother had seen the newsreel in Paisley, having been alerted to it by a neighbour. Here's how James told the story to Craig Curran in 2004:

Oh aye, in the local picture house, the Palaceum in Shettleston them that knew me told my mother that I'd been seen in the Palaceum in a film, she went over but it had been taken to another hall in Paisley and they gave her a line and she went to Paisley and got the photo, the picture, and when I came home she had it. And of course I went to one of the big chemist shops and got a lot of them made. At the end of the war altogether, the Spanish war, when them that was left came home, I could give them the photos. […] There was a big meeting held in the hall in the Calton with the ones that were still living that had been in Spain and […] everybody wanted a photo and I got more made out the chemist shop. Just like a postcard.

After these short stops in temporary holding places, the prisoners were moved to a more secure site. They were taken in the middle of May to the Model Prison at Salamanca, where they were charged with 'aiding military rebellion'. The day they arrived at Salamanca 37 Spaniards were executed as well as German and Russian International Brigaders:

Well after a while we got taken then to a big prison, Salamanca. Which was a real prison. And that's where we were there for a while. […] You see in April 1937 we heard that there had been a big battle at, eh, Guadalajara. And the Russian planes had done that and the Italians had suffered a big reverse. And there was some talk later on that there were some of us going to be exchanged for some of the Italians.

A visit from the British Consul suggested something was afoot:

Well we could understand a bit of Spanish in the papers. The Russians had inflicted a big defeat on the Italians. The Russian bombers had wiped a lot of them out and there was a possibility of us being exchanged for men who had been captured. Well that came true through time and then we got repatriated and we were told we were going home. And gradually, it took a while before we went home, but soon we moved from one place to another up nearer the border with France.

James's impression of Salamanca was that it was built to last and meant to hold them there for a while:

The other ones weren't real prisons. Likesay, the one we were in, the big barn, we had to go out to the street with the big barrel, and put the suction down the well, in the street, and then bring up the water and the water was like, it smelt of petrol and that, you know. And then, in the big barn, with the hundred men, the Spaniards, including ourselves, we had a big, big drum, which was used for urinating in. And it lay there all night till the following morning, and two Spaniards would come in, guards, and carry it out, to empty it. And then the food would come in, in a big drum, for the whole lot of us. And we'd line up with our plate, and get it filled up. And in the morning you'd get what you called a loaf of pan, and that was for to do you for the following morning. But I'll tell you what we could do. The Spaniards themselves, some of the soldiers, they didn't have good footwear. I'm talking about the other side now. And we had got these good army boots. So some of them started to sell their boots – to the Spaniards [Laughs]. Oh they got, aye. And so they could buy something. Well I kept mine as long as I could. And then [...] I decided one time I'd have a feast. And I sold mine. And I sat down one night to a big plate and it was filled wi goat's milk and roe eggs. [...] And I ate that. [...] And then you could also get orange marmalade, maraca. See, you could use your boots that way. I mean actually the Spaniards could have took the boots off us. [Laughs] And gave us nothing. I'll admit that was honesty, on their side. I mean the guards, they could have took the boots off us, what could we have done?

Never one to complain about hardship, and at times James even presented his captors in a reasonably fair light:

The warders were, you know the Spaniards weren't bad. Except

there was one farm, I went up by this farm and there was this
soldier, he was in uniform. And I walked by, I was singing this song
(de di diddle dum) (laughs). He shouted at me and shook his fist,
he wasn't pleased. But the rest of the Spaniards, the ones that were
in charge of us, they were good to us. Right away they started this
thing, we'll buy your shoes. You could send out for huevos, that's
eggs, goat's milk, cigarettes, or whatever you wanted. Some of them
sold their boots... [...] You see I didn't smoke.

He referred to this event in the interview with Conrad Wood in slightly
more detail:

I'd went out, the toilet outside was like a big, I don't know what it
was but it was a big round place with an opening, and it was a lot
of stones with a gap between them [...] Well that was where we did
wur needs. [...] well I was coming back one time from the toilet
and the guard was at the door and I, without knowing it I was
singing the Spanish songs [Laughs]. And I just, I got to the door.
[Laughs] I looked, and he's looking at me. He probably thought
I was mad. [...] The Capitan was a laugh; he had his hair dyed
green. [...] It was green. Aye, the Capitan. Naw, I had a lot of good
laughs in Spain, aye, a lot of good times tae, even as a prisoner.

James finally got word he'd be going home in May 1937. The Italian
defeat at Guadalajara in March had made possible a prisoner exchange,
and the Jarama captives were released, crossing the border into France on
30 May 1937. The prisoners had been in captivity for three months.

We got word we were being exchanged... Well as far as we know
we got exchanged for some of the Italians. And we left there just
quite simple, quite easy. We never had any bother leaving there.
We came right through... Aw well Burgos, Valladolid, and right
through to Irun. And from Irun we got off there and we lined up
and we marched across the bridge. [...] And when we got halfway
across the French met us. That was from Irun into Bayonne.

The men were fingerprinted before being released. On his return to

Glasgow James and the other volunteers were recognised as having some value as recruiters and educators:

> When I came home, I was asked to go to London to do a bit of speaking. As a speaker, you know. […] The Communist Party. See, me being a speaker, but I didn't go to London because, eh, the one I was going to go wi… to London with… I didn't fancy him too much. While we'd been in prison. And eh… Well he'd been trying tae make out that, well, we'd been sort of kidded on when we went over there that our side was winning. [Laughs] And I told him that if our side had been winning we wouldn't have been going over there. Told him we only went because we were needed. But that's how things go. But I did all my own speaking where I lived. In Shettleston and that. I mean I believe in speaking locally. If everybody does their own place then…

When James spoke publicly, often on a platform he carried under his own arm, he spoke of the reasons he went to Spain, the importance of Aid for Spain, the situation of the war, and the value of making the war in Spain last longer to give the antifascists more time to get ready for the struggle ahead:

> Well I knew that the working class in Spain had taken power. And if they could have held onto power for long enough, they'd have made a hell of a difference to other countries possibly round about them.

James considered going back to Spain, but his mother asked him not to. She had already lost four sons and did not want to lose a fifth, so he honoured her wishes. Harold Fry did go back to Spain, the day before his son was born. He was appointed Commander of the British Battalion on 29 September 1937 and died at the Ebro on 13 October. Jimmy Rutherford, another volunteer taken prisoner at Jarama, went back too, and was executed by firing squad on 24 May 1938, aged 20.

Although the Republic was defeated, James saw the intervention of the International Brigades as crucial:

> Well […] we proved the question that if you want to get what you want, you have to fight for it. We fought. The government was

in, the rebel government was in, and we were going to defend the government that had got into power. Now, as you'll remember rightly, Hitler came to power. Now Hitler came to power because, now Hitler went about for years before the war. And it came to the point where the Communist Party got six million votes in Germany [...] The Reichswehr recognised the dangers. Hindenburg, right Hitler, you're in power. Now in his crowd were what you call the Brownshirts, sort of working-class ones that had joined them. The first thing he did was, right, he wiped out the leaders of the Brownshirts. That just left the men. You know what like men are at work. And he was in power, nobody invaded Hitler, nobody invaded Germany. He was in power.

James recognised the impact of non-intervention at a time when Germany and Italy were bolstering Franco:

Oh aye, the Spaniards were good, it's just too bad they got beat. They wouldn't have got beat. You see Britain and France remained neutral, or were supposed to be neutral. And Germany and Italy were nearer Spain than Russia. The rich are hard to beat. That's one thing I'll say about the rich. They'll fight for what they want. But the working class is divided.

When war broke out in 1939, James tried to enlist but was rejected because he was a communist who had been in Spain. At the beginning of November 1940 he was sent to work at Parkhead Forge as a bricklayer's labourer. On Sunday 6 April 1941, a meeting of the workers was called at a church hall in Westmuir Street in Parkhead, and James, by then a well-known agitator and activist, became chairman of the strike committee. Four weeks later the union put a ban on overtime and the furnaces started to run down. On 9 June 1941, James called a strike at Parkhead Forge as Chief Mover, helping to bring 2,000 men out on strike. The strike extended to two other factories, at Dalziel in Motherwell and at Glengarnock. A short time later, having headed down to Ayr for a holiday on the Saturday, James received a telegram telling him to come back to the Forge. The bonus was being granted and he had to try and start a shift.

Then global events took a fresh turn. The Soviet Union came into the war after Germany launched Operation Barbarossa, the biggest invasion in history, on Sunday 22 June 1941. That changed the dynamic for members of the Communist Party, as the Soviet Union was now an ally. When the Russians joined the battle, British communists signed up, and James joined the Royal Artillery, did his three months' training, then volunteered for overseas service. He was posted to India.

James was influenced by two communists from Indian backgrounds. The first was Bombay-born Shapurji Saklatvala (1874–1936), who joined the Communist Party of Great Britain (CPGB) shortly after its formation in 1921. He was elected as Labour MP for Battersea North in 1922 and Communist MP for the same constituency in 1924. For the next five years he was the only Communist Member of Parliament, and the issue of Indian independence was a topic he returned to. Saklatvala lost his seat at the 1929 General Election. He stood as the Communist candidate at the Glasgow Shettleston by-election in June 1930, James's constituency, but lost. Saklatvala died in January 1936, six months before the outbreak of the Spanish Civil War. On 24 December 1936, the week James went to Spain, The *Daily Worker* declared that the British volunteers to fight Franco would be named the Saklatvala Battalion in honour of this esteemed comrade.

The other influential figure was Rajani Palme Dutt (1896–1974), born in Cambridge to a Bengali father and Swedish mother. Like Saklatvala, R Palme Dutt joined the CPGB upon its foundation. Dutt was an expert on India and had considerable influence with the Communist Party of India (CPI) and its complex history there. His book *Modern India* was published in Bombay in 1926. His biographer, John Callaghan, explains Dutt's pivotal role in the CPGB in the wake of the Spanish Civil War and the commencement of the Second World War:

> When Stalin instructed the world communist movement to characterise the war as imperialist and unjust on both sides, [Harry] Pollitt was unable to comply and Dutt took over the general secretaryship (until the Nazi invasion of Russia in June 1941 when Pollitt was reinstated).

James adhered to the anti-imperialist line laid out by Dutt, and did not enlist until 1941, partly because, as I've mentioned, communists who had fought in Spain were viewed with suspicion by the British Army. Meanwhile in India in 1940–41, the British had interned without trial hundreds of communists under the 1939 Defence of India Act, an updated version of a draconian imperial measure that dated from World War One. This is the context in which James arrived in Bombay, as a soldier and a communist, and as someone who shared the view that the war was about Empire. When Singapore fell, with Gandhi and Nehru against the war, Britain had to look to the communists in India. Yet when he arrived in Bombay, James found that Communist Party members were in prison despite Russia now being in the war. He made contact with some of those newly released from prison and took part in a public debate about the causes of the war with an army captain, at the end of which he was met by two military police. James recalled the circumstances of his arrival in India in the wake of the sinking of a British battleship and battlecruiser in the South China Sea on 10 December 1941:

We were sailing to Singapore when news came through that the Japanese were in occupation. They had also attacked and sunk two of our ships, *The Prince of Wales* and *The Repulse*. Our troop ship was diverted to India. While in Bombay a mate and I, on a day pass, got caught in very heavy rain. Think we get deluges in Scotland? This was a waterfall pouring from the sky! Everyone raced for shelter. Two ladies in a rickshaw hesitated about stepping into the rushing torrent on the street. So us two Glasgow gentlemen approached and carried them into the hotel foyer. Turns out they were Scots. Officers' wives who had been brought to Bombay to wait for a passage home. Their husbands were missing in Malaya. Because of the war situation we had not been receiving mail from home and reckoned that our families were not getting our letters. The ladies took our addresses and promised to write to our folks when they got home to Scotland. I later found that the promise had been kept and our folks appreciated the assurance that we were safe and well. It was a good thing that they did, considering their own grief and worry over their missing menfolk. Soon we were on the move again. On the road to Burma, but that is another story.

While he was in Bombay, on Marine Drive, he went to meetings in uniform and was invited by students to speak to them in their hall. He saw the women walk up and down in threes with the Indian flag. The struggle for independence was on hold for the war but it was unstoppable.

In Darjeeling in 1944, James met a British soldier who had also been in the Communist Party. This soldier introduced him to a man who worked in Lloyds Bank in Darjeeling and organised a meeting attended by around 300 people. James spoke at this meeting about the war and recited some verses of a little song he used to sing with his comrades, which he knew by heart. It was Joe Hill's 'Should I Ever be a Soldier', first published in 1913:

Should I ever be a soldier/ 'Neath the Red Flag I would fight/
Should a gun I ever shoulder/ It will be to crush the tyrant's might/
Join the army of the toilers/ Men and women fall in line/ Workers
of the world unite/ And do your duty in the fight for liberty.

James was upfront about his agitation, and he later reflected that this helped him get away with it. He never skulked around or allowed himself to be embarrassed or anxious about possible surveillance:

I found out that, as long as I went the way I did about it, they
didn't come near me. You see, I didn't show any fear. The
Communist Party had been made legal.

Anti-communism was bred in the bones of the British authorities, but with Russia now an ally, being a Communist was beginning to have different connotations to those it had in the 1930s. Another large meeting James spoke at was in Bangalore, where he addressed 700 British troops of all ranks:

Sherwood Foresters, Durham Light Infantry, Cameronians,
Gordons, and I spoke there for two hours to these soldiers. I was
up for posting the next morning to the 6th Punjabs. Well I went
round and saw the captain and I got it rescinded. I took the whole
thing in my stride.

James never joined the 6th Punjabs, but he did go on to serve with the 2nd Battalion of the King's Own Scottish Borderers. Flying to Kamila in March 1945, James spoke to a soldier who was anti-communist, and took him to a small bookshop where he bought some pamphlets. A short time later James was confronted by two Military Policemen (MPs):

I said to them is it this stuff here, I said. I said I'm a member of the Communist Party, and they're looking at me and looking at each other, and you see they saw there was no fear. No, it's all right. So I went back the following day, the following morning myself to the bookshop, I went in, and the man said, 'The district commissioner of police was in here asking about you'. I said look, what's he gonnae do? You're a legal party now. You're not... you're legal, you've got a flag flying up there. Don't worry I said, they can do nothing to me. What are they gonnae do? That was all. You know, I never had any hard truck from the British Army either, even the officers they knew me, just said to me, 'We know about you.' One colonel said to me, 'I don't know whether you can walk, but,' he said, 'By Christ, you can talk!' No, I would never grumble against the British Army neither, I couldnae grumble. I'm no a grumbler in that line.

James moved from Kamila through Chan into Prome, Mandalay, and Rangoon. He was in one of the toughest war zones of the time and was fortunate to come through unscathed:

I was lucky in a sense, and some soldiers were unlucky. The day they were moving up there was a bunch from Hamilton and you know they all got killed in the one day. You see, I went up a couple of days after them. It was big fields, you know what like big fields are, it would be fenced off and other fields, and all fields, well I blame them who were in charge, they all came from Hamilton. They went across this field, they couldn't see a thing, there could have been a hundred men on the other side of the field behind the hedges, they got bumped off. You see it's like this house here, you go from here, and there's a wall up here, and you don't know what's on the other side of that wall, or that wall. Instead of branching out and put a man on another field, then one man going forward himself, right up to the top in each field, then you know whether there's anybody there or not. See it's what you call dead ground. What you can't see is dangerous.

In his first action James was made a Lance Corporal but in the interview with Conrad Wood in 1991 he recalls that he had this rank removed when the war was ending, probably for insubordination, since that was his trademark:

> I got the tape taken off me, but I didn't bother about the tape. What did I want tape for? But, em, I had a good time in… When I came out of action in June '45, after three months, and eh, this chap's going down to the 14th CCS Hospital [Casualty Clearing Station], came from Springburn, and I went with him and the nurse said to the matron, she said, 'Eh, are yous with the KOSBS?' I said 'Yes.' She said, 'Eh, would you like a wee job here?' So I got a job dishing out to a hundred men mepacrine tablets, sulfamide and everything else in this hospital. And I was told, well, each man gets a bottle of beer a day, and cigarettes. And then there was bottles of lime juice and that, that got dished out. Well anybody who was in the Queen's, the South Lancs or the KOSBS got an extra bottle of beer [laughs]. I had six every day. I was … instead of claiming for a hundred men, I claimed for a hundred and fifty [laughs again]. And that was the army. And I lay out in the sun there […] and when they sent word ower after seven weeks for I was going home, I didnae feel like going home [laughs]. Actually I could have stayed there for life.

George Orwell shared with James Maley the experience of fighting in Spain in 1937: Orwell as a member of POUM (Partido Obrero de Unificación Marxista) and Maley as a member of the Communist Party. It's a long way from the mean streets of Glasgow's East End to the playing fields of Eton, but history is full of strange bedfellows. And they had something else in common – an experience of empire. Orwell was born Eric Blair in Bengal in 1903. James served in India during the Second World War as a gunner with the Royal Artillery. Both men also served in Burma. Orwell arrived in Rangoon on 27 November 1922 at the age of 19 as an Assistant Superintendent of Police. Eton could get you quite far in those days too. James arrived as a soldier with the 2nd Battalion King's Own Scottish Borderers 20 years later.

Other than the newsreel images in a prison yard after being captured at Jarama, there were only a few other photos of James during this period of his life. One photo that later captured the attention of his children was of James shooting a tiger. It was a fake photo, taken in a studio in India,

James Maley takes aim at a stuffed tiger for a studio portrait in a rare moment of calm during his Far East service.

with him pointing a rifle at a stuffed tiger. There was another staged picture of his time in India and Burma, this time posing as a boxer with another soldier. He occasionally came up with memorable anecdotes, such as his description of drinking water from the Irrawaddy River while dead bodies floated past, stories of sniper fire and malaria, and killing; lots of killing. Beyond this, though, little was passed on about his experiences in India and Burma. The earliest and in fact the only piece of handwriting the family have from James is a letter he sent from India where he was serving with an anti-aircraft battery of the Royal Artillery. The letter, dated Tuesday 25 January 1944 is addressed to his sister Annie:

Dear Sister,

I have just received your letter dated 5.1.44, I also got two lots of papers *Sunday Mail, Post, Weekly News*, and *Standard*. I see you went to the Alhambra to see *Red Riding Hood* you would also see Willie there doing his stuff. As you say things are changing back home, Annie eating like a horse, Jim starting to play football, and Teresa getting bigger every day. You say you are sending some cigs, well it is too late to tell you now but they are best sent packed in tins, instead of packets, as on the long sea voyage they are apt to get damp. I am going to send you some more tea and sugar when I get the chance, but I am still waiting to hear that you received the last one, also if the shoe's have arrived. That's all for the present so write soon, and send plenty of news.

Love to All, JM

Marriage and Family

After he came home from Burma James didn't do any more public speaking. He recognised a change in the working class in Britain and realised that the Labour Party – for which he never had any time – was here to stay. James worked in Maryhill Barracks as a telephone operator until 1947, never staying at the barracks but walking home each night to his mother's house in Shettleston. In 1947, he left the army and applied for a job at the Telecom Office in George Street. He didn't get the job and left with the impression that he had the right experience but the wrong name and the wrong religion. He half-wished he had stayed in the army long enough to have that interview, since he sensed that being in uniform might have offset any anti-Catholicism. This discrimination was something he experienced later working on the railway and for Glasgow Corporation as a labourer. In addition to covert blacklisting of men who fought in Spain, James added his own experiences of being passed over for work after the war due to anti-Catholicism. He was a Red to the Catholic Church and a 'Fenian' to the bigots.

Early in 1949, James went to the Highlanders' Institute, a popular social venue at 27 Elmbank Street in Glasgow, where he met his future bride. James was 40 years old and had a rich life behind him. Anne Watt, born in Roslin Place in Cowcaddens and living at the time with her mother in Mansion Street in Possilpark, was 26 and had been on the Kintyre coast during the war as a Land Girl. James asked Anne to dance and danced her to the end of life. They didn't exchange addresses or telephone numbers but arranged to meet at Boots Corner in Argyle Street the following Saturday. James was late getting back from a Celtic match in Dundee (probably the Scottish Cup First Round game with Dundee United which Celtic lost 4-3) but Anne patiently waited at the notorious 'Dizzy Corner'. She never had to wait for him again. James was ready to settle down. He had found the love of his life and proposed within two weeks of their meeting. On Friday 25 March 1949 they were married at Henry Drummond Church in Possilpark. By then he was a railway-track layer and she was a shirt cutter. Friends had told her she would be a young widow since she was marrying an older man, but they were wrong. He was a one-woman man, a one-party man, and one of a kind. James could be dogmatic – his mother recommended to Anne that she use a frying pan on his head if he got out of hand – but he and Anne were a pair of lovebirds. Having been one of nine children, James became a father of nine. Within the next 14 years, he and Anne had five daughters – Barbara, Cathy, Marina, Anne and Patricia – followed by four sons – Jimmy, Willy, John and Eddy. Although he never smoked or drank, never spent time in pubs or clubs, never socialised with friends outside of the house, James was the life and soul of his family, and a popular local presence in Possilpark, active in the Tenants' Association, in the Communist Party, and in the scheme. He walked everywhere and knew everybody.

In the 1950s James worked with the Permanentway Relay squads out of Shettleston depot and was a member of the NUR. One story he told was of him and his brother going for a walk in the middle of the night on their break near the leafy suburb of Milngavie and getting stopped by the cops after someone reported two suspicious men in bunnets wandering the streets.

James remained a member of the Communist Party, attended meetings and rallies, bought the *Daily Worker* and, when the title changed to the *Morning Star* in 1966, continued to buy that paper and as much of the socialist press and pamphlets as he could get his hands on. There were plenty of left-wing bookshops in Glasgow at the time – Clyde Books on Parnie Street was a favourite haunt, and Calton Books on London Road is one of the last remaining outposts.

Although James was raised a Catholic, and was a lifelong supporter of Celtic FC, his children went to non-denominational schools. Once, a priest came to the door asking after this big family with the Irish surname, muttering the word 'turncoat'. James's take on religion was to say that he 'couldn't be in heaven knowing there was one person in hell'. He brought up the children to be avid readers and self-educators like him, borrowing books from the Book Exchange at Gilmorehill near to the University and giving them a week to read them before taking them back in return for others. The small bookshelf never expanded, but the reading list was long and rich and better than anything to be had at school. The collected works of Marx and Lenin and Mao sat alongside Dickens, Agatha Christie, and Harold Robbins. His other loves included walking and whistling. In later years he swapped a bunnet for a baseball cap and seemed to have rediscovered his youth. Richard Baxell has remarked that

> James Maley appears in both my accounts of the British volunteers in the Spanish Civil War and there is also an interview with him in the Imperial War Museum. He received fulsome obituaries following his death in 2007.

But the fact is that James was invisible in print for over 50 years after coming home from Spain. As a teetotaller looking after a big family in a poor neighbourhood on a low wage with no phone in the house, he slipped under the radar. He never drove a car and seldom travelled. James was an internationalist, yet his international travels were few and far between. He was first abroad as a 21-year-old in Cleveland Ohio, then in Spain in 1937, then Burma and India in 1941–45, then back to Spain for a commemorative event in 1996. He travelled in other ways though, always reading the international socialist press, selling the *Daily Worker* and the Morning Star, and subscribing to the *Soviet Weekly* and *Beijing Review*.

The fact that he got noticed in his latter years was at least partly due to my brother John and I writing a play based on his experiences. I always had the feeling he had been slighted and for three reasons. First, because he never looked for attention. Second, because he lived in the present and was always more interested in what was going on day-to-day than dwelling on the past. For him the struggle was there every day. Third, he had no time for time-servers and Labour Party careerists. He never moved from his roots in the Communist Party from the day he joined in 1932. He kept the faith when others lost theirs. There is also another factor: James was, in the words of one of his grandsons, 'a thrawn bugger', meaning he was a difficult and demanding character who had little time for sentiment.

James attended an event in 1989 to unveil a plaque to William Keegan, an ex-miner from Baillieston in Glasgow who had died at the Battle of Brunete on 18 July 1937. At the civilised tea and biscuits that followed James, still a communist, argued with the Labour Party members and representatives present who had organised the ceremony. He was always critical of those he saw as careerists or opportunists. One of his hosts said, 'Oh James, you're like a bear with a burnt arse!' This was such an apt description that the line made its way into *From the Calton to Catalonia*. That play appeared in 1990, when Glasgow was supposed to be celebrating its year as European City of Culture with a glossy makeover, and the city council faced opposition from socialists insisting that this was a Workers' City. This was a clash between two traditions, Glasgow as Second City of the Empire and Glasgow as the hub of Red Clydeside. From the Calton to Catalonia was first staged at the Pearce Institute in Govan from 3–7 December 1990. The play was still being performed as recently as 2018.

At that opening week, there were some interesting encounters. A Moroccan postgraduate student at Strathclyde University where I was teaching at the time told me after a performance that his own father had fought for Franco as one of the 'African jackals' that Pablo Neruda and others had disparaged, and whose supposed cruelty the International Brigades had feared. Paul Preston, a leading authority on Spain, suggested in 2004 that the Spanish Civil War was also a colonial conflict. What Preston made clear was that understanding Spanish history and the colonial situation in Morocco was essential to making sense of what happened in 1936. Another post-performance audience encounter in 1990 was with a man aged 65 who, as a boy of 12 in 1937, the year in which the play was set, had collected Food for Spain with his mother in the Gorbals. One of the scenes in the play depicts two women with a pram collecting food for Spain, and this had triggered the man's memory.

In 1996 James went back to Spain with his eldest son, Jimmy, for the first time in 60 years, and was interviewed there by Reevel Alderson for BBC Radio 5. In 2004 Craig Curran conducted the interview that would later, together with Conrad Wood's earlier interview, form the basis for preserving his memories of Spain. In 2006 the last photos for the press were taken, 70 years on from 1936. That same summer, after a preliminary scoping interview for *An Anarchist's Story*, scripted by Chris Dolan, the filmmakers decided not to interview James due to his accent, and perhaps also because of his communist politics, given that the film's focus was on the anarchist journalist Ethel MacDonald. Walking down from the sheltered housing where the filmmakers had spoken to James and overhearing them resolve not to include him in the film, I felt sad. When the documentary was screened on BBC 2 Scotland on 24 January 2007, it struck me that the living testimony of someone who had actually been in Spain was missing.

James kept good health for most of his adult life but fell ill on the morning of Saturday 7 April 2007. He was hospitalised later that afternoon and the family gathered round his bedside in the Western Infirmary. Just after midnight on Easter Monday, 9 April 2007, he passed away, aged 99. A few days before he died, his granddaughter was cutting his hair before she left for a holiday in Spain, and she was pleased to hear that he remembered some phrases in Spanish from his time in captivity seventy years earlier. It turned out he knew a lot more of the language than 'No Pasaran!' The death certificate gave the cause of death as pneumonia. Eighty years down the line, the illness that he had fought off in 1926 came back for him. The certificate gave his occupation as 'Builder's Labourer (retired)', but that was only his final waged employment. He had done so much more. When James was interviewed by Craig Curran in 2004 his last words were 'I'm a soldier.' He was. There was always a war on for him, with the class war the most constant conflict.

Legacy

I taught two seminars on Shakespeare the day after my father died. That seemed surreal, as was the fact that Barclay McBain, an editor at *The Herald*, asked me to write my father's obituary. I knew Barclay, having written for the newspaper previously, but the request would have struck me as odd if I wasn't already in shock, like all the family. Although my father was 99 when he died he was always all there. He went into the shower the morning he took ill, and when the ambulance arrived at the hospital and he came out on the stretcher he said, 'We're on the move,' as though he was going into battle. My obituary for my father was one of the 'fulsome obituaries' mentioned by Richard Baxell. Others appeared in *The Scotsman* (Jim Gilchrist) and *The Independent* (Jim Jump). In my tribute I said that my father's communism owed more to the Calton than to the Kremlin and I meant it. Grassroots activism starts at home, and Glasgow's East End was a seedbed for revolutionary socialism. Being asked to write my father's obituary meant I had the makings of his eulogy too, which I drafted for the humanist celebrant.

Scottish Television (STV) asked if they could film the funeral, since my father was an historical figure, and at that time the oldest-surviving

Scottish member of the International Brigades, not the last left alive but the oldest combatant. The Green Brigade, the Celtic FC ultras, asked to bring a banner up to the crematorium. In the end none of this happened. It was kept as a private family affair. But when Celtic played St Johnstone in the semi-final of the Scottish Cup at Hampden on the afternoon of Saturday 14 April 2007, the day of my father's funeral, the Green Brigade unfurled banners in his memory: 'R.I.P. James Maley' and 'No Pasaran!', and a slogan in Scots Gaelic that said: 'Racism Out'. At Maryhill Crematorium the coffin was draped in the banner of the International Brigades and the flag of the Spanish Republic.

Later that month Paul Sheridan and Chris Cruickshank from The Wakes visited me in my office at the University of Glasgow. They had written a song called 'These Hands', based on an article by Paul Dalgarno that had appeared in *The Big Issue* in November 2006. They brought to life my father's words as quoted in that article and as depicted in the photograph that accompanied the piece. Listening to it was a very emotional experience. The song had been completed when news of my father's death reached The Wakes. I'd have loved him to have heard it.

In 2008 Daniel Gray's book about the Scots who fought Franco appeared. *Homage to Caledonia* includes an interview with Steve Fullarton, who recalled my father's speeches:

> I always attended his meetings. The Communist Party organiser would say 'it's time we had a meeting' at the Cross, Shettleston Cross. If Jimmy was available, he would always go. So Jimmy would carry this collapsible platform up to Shettleston Cross and I would give a hand to take it up there. Or, sometimes it was to help with chalking the streets, announcing that tomorrow night there would be a meeting by the Communist Party and Jimmy Maley would be speaking. We would write on the road – the road was smooth – and we chalked everywhere. Sometimes we painted it with whitewash; the traffic was such then that you could do that. Jimmy Maley was a provocative speaker. He knew that the Catholic young men would be there in force, repeating whatever lies had been issued to them from the chapel. They would come out with these ridiculous things, even too ridiculous to bother about. Jimmy didn't worry about that. Jimmy would be right in there and would knock the feet from them, would leave them speechless.

Around the same time, 2007–08, filmmaker Don Coutts unearthed tapes from the early 1990s of interviews with members of the International Brigades, including James. These interviews were edited and appeared as part of *The Scots Who Fought Franco*, a two-part documentary series narrated by actor David Hayman, which aired on 13 August and 20 August 2009.

On 12 October 2011, I hosted a one-day event at The Mitchell Theatre entitled 'Fighting Franco, Fighting Fascism', and it was here that the seeds for this current book were sown. Stuart Christie, author of *Granny Made Me An Anarchist*, was the only speaker there that day who had actually fought Franco in his own lifetime. Arrested in Madrid in August 1964, aged 18, and charged with being part of a plot to blow up the Spanish dictator at the Santiago Bernabéu Stadium during the final of the Generalissimo's Cup, Christie had avoided execution. The penalty, had it been carried out, was death by garrote, which involved slow strangulation by an iron collar, topped off by a bolt through the back of the neck. I knew and admired Stuart. When he reviewed *Homage to Caledonia*, in 2009, Stuart demonstrated characteristic generosity of spirit. It would have been easy for him, given his strong anarchist sentiments, to call out the communists as dupes or stooges, as some anti-communist commentators like to do. He was able to see the bigger picture when reflecting on the commitment and sacrifice of men like my father.

> The selfless men and women who fought in Spain for the idea of
> liberty against the reactionary priest-, gun- and prison-backed,
> medieval ideology that was Francoism are the forgotten dead
> and a now-dying generation to whom we have an obligation of
> remembrance.

Other speakers at The Mitchell that day included Rosemary Williams, named Rosemary for remembrance because she was born while her father, Archibald 'AC' Williams was in the same Spanish prison as James Maley after their capture at Jarama; George Park, son of Alec Park, who died at the Aragon Front; Allan Craig from Maryhill, whose father Allan died at Jarama; William Crawford, grandson of William, who died at Jarama; Geraldine Abrahams and Anne O'Hara, daughters of Gerry Doran, wounded at Cordoba; Jennie Renton, daughter of Donald Renton, captured at Jarama; and Norman Dunlop, son of John Dunlop, wounded at Brunete.

The following year, on 17 March 2012, I chaired a literary event attended by 400 people at The Mitchell Theatre to discuss with Paul Preston his new book, *The Spanish Holocaust*. In 2015 Craig Curran's interview resurfaced and was digitised, transcribed and posted on YouTube. In 2016 Fair Pley Theatre Company started rehearsed readings of *From the Calton to Catalonia*, which ran for the next two years. Memory is a living thing. I was amazed when Rosemary Williams showed me the prison notebook her father had kept, which showed that the men had occupied themselves in some of the ways John and I had suggested in *From the Calton to Catalonia* – helping each other to pass the time in captivity. On 27 August 2011, at the unveiling of a statue of a Spanish bull on Renton Main Street in memory of Dunbartonshire volunteers, I spoke with Alex Dewar, who was three when his father, Archie, from Aberdeen, died at the Aragon Front. Later still, at an event on Clydeside at the statue of La Pasionaria, I met Tam Watters, and realised how much we had in common, far more than the fact that our fathers fought Franco.

I grew up with those two pictures from my father's time in Spain, cut from the newsreel from 23 March 1937, one showing him front right on the back of a lorryload of captured comrades, and one in a prison yard, standing in the same position. I watched the newsreel from which those two frames were cut in its original format for the first time on the 27 of September 2020 when Tam Watters, whose father Geordie was imprisoned alongside mine, sent me a copy. A few days later I came across an image online that must have come from another newsreel that shows my father walking down a street with his comrades and fellow prisoners. I suspect there's more material out there.

I started to read more of the history, including the anarchist and socialist versions, reading like a scholar rather than a son. It didn't change my opinion of my father's role in that struggle, but it made me see how sentimentalism and sectarianism could conceal the complexities that shaped the period. It's hard to imagine now that people without any internet, without any university education, or any advanced schooling, had access to the kind of anti-imperialist internationalist literature that, after the Russian

Memorial to Dunbartonshire IB volunteers, Renton Main Street.

Artist Arthur Dooley's sculpture on Clydeside erected in memory of Dolores Ibárruri Gómez, 'La Pasionaria', a Republican leader during the Spanish Civil War.

Revolution, the Communist Party was providing. James remained a committed socialist and internationalist to the end, but he was passionately interested in what was happening in the here-and-now. The week before he died he had the atlas out when I visited and showed me Sudan on the map. Something was brewing in this part of the world and he was animated and eager to talk.

Many Scots were and still are socialists and internationalists, republicans and anti-imperialists. They don't hold with invading and occupying countries; theirs is a spirit of radical resistance and international solidarity. Eighty-five years down the line that same fighting spirit, that same rage against injustice, and that same hope for a better future persists. And the threat's still there – the danger of fascism and the risk of forgetting the lessons of the past. In many ways the Spanish Civil War is still going on, and not just in terms of legacy, memory and missing persons. Historians continue to take sides. Anarchists, Trotskyists, socialists and communists fight the same battles over and over. Was it a Revolution betrayed by the Soviet Union or a Republic in need of defending? Was it the prelude to World War 2 or another colonial episode in a long history of European imperialism? In an article in *The Guardian* on 7 May 2017, Paul Preston observed:

> Eighty years ago this week, the Ramblas of Barcelona echoed
> with gunfire. Much of what happened on the streets during the
> May days is well known thanks to George Orwell's *Homage to
> Catalonia*, but not why it happened.

Preston calls Orwell's book 'another nail in the communist coffin, despite its distortion of the Spanish situation'. But Orwell can be seen in a different light, as Preston himself acknowledges. In July 1937, Orwell wrote: 'The International Brigade is in some sense fighting for all of us – a thin line of suffering and often ill-armed human beings standing between barbarism and at least comparative decency.'

As the last members of the International Brigades pass away, there's a sense of brushing the coat-tails of history. The Spanish Civil War is still an open book – and an open wound. Despite innumerable studies of causes, courses, consequences, it's too early to say what happened between July 1936 and April 1939, and after, beyond Franco's dictatorship and death, into the recovery of the memories of those who survived, and the recovery of the bodies of those who did not. Spain remains a crucible of conflict for critics and combatants, and for all those whose lives it affected. Only now in the last light of living memory is the serious business of truth and reconciliation underway, although the fallout from Franco and fascism lingers on. Spain remains a touchstone for the British Left, its finest hour, and yet the place where the seeds of nostalgia, bitterness and failure were sown – sectarianism, sentimentalism, the Cold War, McCarthyism. It was a training ground for the Blitzkrieg and the site of significant advances in battlefield surgery and medicine. It is one of the most mediatised, dramatised, poeticised and novelised wars in history. It is also James Maley's war – not the only one, or the last, but the first and most memorable.

2

DONALD RENTON

Not made with rosewater

Jennie Renton

I AM SITTING in a caravan at Forsay near Glenuig in Moidart, looking over Loch nan Uamh, where Bonnie Prince Charlie is said to have landed in 1745. My father, Donald Renton, had no truck with the romancing of royalty. If he was here, he would denounce its shallow glamour, declaring the prince to be emblematic of pernicious social hierarchy. For Don was a man who, when called upon to fill in an official form, would enter 'communist agitator' under Occupation and 'militant atheist' under Religion; at the bookies, when placing a bet, his moniker was 'Don Red Renton'.

A lifelong Marxist and revolutionary, Don was also a utopian democrat. As a political commissar in the International Brigade, he was lucky that his captors did not realise this when he was taken prisoner during the Battle of Jarama, only a few months after setting foot on Spanish soil in December 1936. His loyalty to the Communist Party of Great Britain was unswerving until the Hungarian Revolution of 1956. It would be no exaggeration to say that his break with the CP broke his heart.

I remember going into our local paper shop when I was about eight and being told, 'Let your father know he has to come in and pay for these.' The newsagent gestured to a stack of *Daily Worker* newspapers as tall as me, piled up behind the counter. I felt tongue-tied and anxious at the sight.

Much later, I learned that Don, until then a full-time and fully committed CP organiser, had taken vehement exception to the treatment of the *Worker*

Hungary correspondent, 29-year-old Peter Fryer, whose reports on how the revolution was being crushed by the Soviet army were rejected for publication. Refusing to be silenced, Fryer wrote *Hungarian Tragedy* and on its publication was expelled from the Party.

Don quit the Communist Party over Hungary.

The impulse to build a fairer world was what drew my dad to join the Communist Party as a teenager. His essential humanity took him, in the years beyond the CP, into the Labour Party, where he devoted his energies as an Edinburgh councillor to causes such as better social housing and was one of the group of people who helped Helen Crummy to start the Craigmillar Festival Society.

On the longest seat of the caravan at Forsay, I have spread out papers relating to my dad's life. Among them is a pile of 'Don Renton's Column' from the *Tribune*. A couple of months ago, the historian Owen Dudley Edwards dropped into my bookshop to let me know he had come across these, published in the late 1930s, during his researches in the National Library of Scotland. I didn't know that Don had been a *Tribune* writer – none of these columns had been clipped out and put into the big ledger of cuttings from the 1930s which I had pored over so many times as a little girl. Owen kindly made photocopies at the library and brought them to me.

As I look through them now, I realise how to approach writing this chapter. I want to give an idea of the range and trajectory of Don's political activities throughout his life; to contextualise his experience as an International Brigader; to show what he was fighting *for*, not just what he was fighting against.

I open the worn ledger which has accompanied me through life. The cuttings, brown with age, are mostly from the late 1930s – how delicate the newsprint has become. There are grainy photographs of men in scuffles with police, blocking the traffic in the centre of London, chained to railings. Neatly clipped out is a letter published in the *Edinburgh Evening News* in December 1960, in which Don denounces Julian Symons' condescending account of the activities of the National Unemployed Workers' Movement (NUWM) in the Hungry Thirties; Don asserts that 'personal testimony is much more important than the writing of someone who tries to describe incidents after they have taken place'. And so, where possible, Don's own words tell his story here.

Born on 30 March 1912, Don grew up in a tiny flat in Bridge Street,

Portobello, with six brothers and two sisters. His mother, Julia, had been a land worker in East Lothian. His father died when he was 14 and he left school to go out to work and contribute to the meagre family income. An apprenticeship as a painter and decorator (his father's trade) came to an abrupt end when he was fired for using company paint for daubing pavements with political slogans. He was blacklisted for militancy.

Don became well-known in the Portobello area as a political activist, involved in campaigns relating to the local environment, housing and (un) employment. A few years ago, an elderly man came into my bookshop on a mission to tell me that he had been brought up opposite my granny's flat in Mount Lodge Place. He remembers being woken up one evening by the sound of someone singing 'The Internationale' in the street. His mother, less than pleased at her little boy arising prematurely from his slumbers, told him that it was just Donald Renton giving it laldy, and to get back to sleep.

By the age of 17 Don was a convinced communist. He was inspired by radical speakers he heard at the foot of The Mound – where right up to the 1970s people of every ideological stripe took to their soapboxes.

In an interview by Ian Wood published in the *Scottish Labour History Journal* in 1977, Don recalls:

> I joined the Labour Party here in Edinburgh in Portobello soon after the General Strike, in which I took part. The timidity and treachery of the MacDonald-Snowden leadership in face of a capitalist crisis which threw thousands onto the dole drove me and many others out of the party, and I joined the Communist Party in 1929, and was a member until the crushing of the Hungarian rising in 1956. After becoming unemployed myself, I took an active part in the fight for 'work or full maintenance' and got to know Harry McShane and Wal Hannington very well in the National Unemployed Workers' Movement.

In the early 1930s, Don founded the Portobello Branch of the National Unemployed Workers' Movement, taking up the cudgels on behalf of people attempting to appeal against the heartless rulings of the Means Test introduced by the 'National' Government of Ramsay MacDonald in 1931, a time of mass unemployment. The Means Test might have been dreamt up

THE NATIONAL HUNGER
MARCH TO LONDON
1930

WHY WE ARE MARCHING

By
WAL HANNINGTON
(*Organiser of the March*)

Containing also :—
ROUTES and TIMETABLES

PRICE - - 1D.

National Unemployed Workers' Movement, 23 Great
Ormond Street, London, W.C.1

Pamphlet by Wal Hannington giving routes and timetables of the national hunger march to London, 1930.

by Torquemada. Under the guise of fiscal probity, it was more a means of tormenting those who had hit rock bottom. Possession of a radio was deemed sufficient reason to cut off benefit and throw families into deeper crisis and despair. Don's eloquence and ability to mount a cogent argument was sometimes enough to win the day at an Appeal Tribunal. 'They cut unemployment pay by introducing what they called the Anomalies Act, which denied benefit to scores of thousands of unemployed men and women in every part of the country,' Don writes in notes set down decades later. 'This went hand-in-hand with what they called the Not Genuinely Seeking Work Clause and similarly obnoxious methods to deprive claimants of their right to unemployment pay.' In Don's terms, this was class war, plain and simple.

He was also involved in campaigns to provide amenities for tenants in Edinburgh's new council housing areas of Lochend and Niddrie, and to prevent evictions. In what became known as 'The Siege of Gardners' Crescent', he barricaded himself into a first floor flat with a family that had fallen into rent arrears. After holding off the bailiffs for four days, Don was arrested and appeared in court on a charge of breach of the peace. Asked if he had anything to say, he responded: 'A communist never whines for mercy from the puppets who administer justice.' He was sentenced to 30 days.

Don stood three times in local elections in Portobello, a Tory stronghold. In 1935, as election agent for Willie Gallacher, he was at the heart of the brilliantly successful campaign which saw the communist candidate become MP for West Fife. He chaired two packed meetings at the Usher Hall, for Willie Gallacher and Harry Pollitt respectively. The Usher Hall (Edinburgh's main concert hall) was also the venue for two meetings of the British Union of

Benito Mussolini (left), Oswald Mosley (right) in 1936.

Fascists, addressed by Oswald Mosley and his sidekick William Joyce (later known as Lord Haw-Haw for his broadcasts in support of Hitler). Don was in one of the upper galleries when he made his presence known by bursting into 'The Internationale'. Other left-wingers present saw him being brutally bundled around the steeply raked tiers of seating; he was given a kicking all the way until he landed on the street outside, his clothes bloody and ragged. My uncle, Bill Cranston, who also fought in Spain, was in the demonstration outside the Usher Hall. He told me that this wasn't the only time Don had been 'hammered'. Bill once said to me that he wasn't political like my father, that he went to Spain because he saw fascism as wrong and he wanted to do something to stop this evil spreading. Interviewed by that great recorder of working-class memories, Ian Mac-Dougall, he explained that he was always one to make decisions at his own discretion. Don, in the 1930s, put his trust in Moscow.

As an organiser of the hunger marches from Scotland to London, in 1934 and 1936, when he was leader and quartermaster of the Edinburgh contingent, Don threw himself into the fight for work and 'full maintenance for all whom capitalism had denied the right to work'. He was destined to become one of the leaders of the National Unemployed Workers' Movement, closely associated with Wal Hannington and Harry McShane 'in the great pre-war demonstrations against government starvation policies'.

After the 1936 Hunger March, Don volunteered to serve in Spain:

> It was a matter of solidarity with the people of Spain in their struggle
> against reaction in their own country aided by arms and men from
> the fascist powers. But there was more to it than just that – we
> regarded the defence of democracy in Spain as being inseparable
> from the defence of our own homeland against Hitler's drive to
> subjugate all the peoples of Europe.

Don volunteered to join the International Brigade and with 63 others
travelled from Dover to Dunkirk on 20 December 1936. In Paris, the group
boarded a train for Perpignan. At the Spanish border, they 'encountered
no interference from the French police or railway authorities. This was no
doubt due to the election to office of the Popular Front earlier in 1936'.
He was exhilarated by the huge welcome they received in Madrid:

> It is an atmosphere I will never forget – there was the sense of
> freedom in the air, of workers' power, and of course the crushing
> of the Nationalist insurrection was still fresh in people's minds. I
> got some six weeks' training at Madrigueras in Albacete province.
> This began with essential weapons training, the result of Tom
> Wintringham's influence. He was a most effective instructor, who
> believed the importance of coordinated foot-drill would be clear
> to us once we could handle our weapons. In fact, many of those
> drilling us in the British battalion of the xv Brigade had regular
> army experience. In the case of one of them, Jock Cunningham,
> this experience had included serving part of a five-year sentence for
> mutiny while serving with the Argylls in the West Indies.

His first experience of action was on the line of the Jarama river, south
of Madrid, in early February 1937:

> This was the first time the British volunteers saw action together as
> a battalion though many of us had already fought with other units,
> notably the French and German Battalions of the International
> Brigade.

With the goal of cutting the Madrid–Valencia road, Nationalist troops, comprising Spanish Foreign Legion units as well as Moroccan, German and Italian Fascists, ferociously stormed the Jarama line. Don recalls:

We couldn't have been given a more important task. I had been trained to handle machine guns and was Commissar to our battalion's machine-gun company. Fear in a situation like this, when you have not fought before, must be conquered. And as a Commissar I had to show an example. But I was afraid, make no mistake about that.

Don would later wear with pride the scars on his leg caused by dumdum bullets – as a child in the 1950s, I was shown them on a couple of occasions

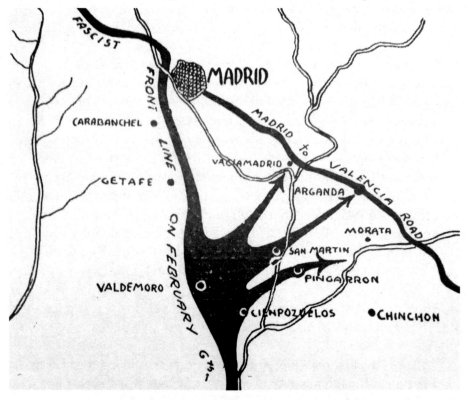

Three-pronged Fascist attack, Battle of Jarama, February 1937.
(Map by Alexander Anderson, from *Records of the XV International Brigade*)

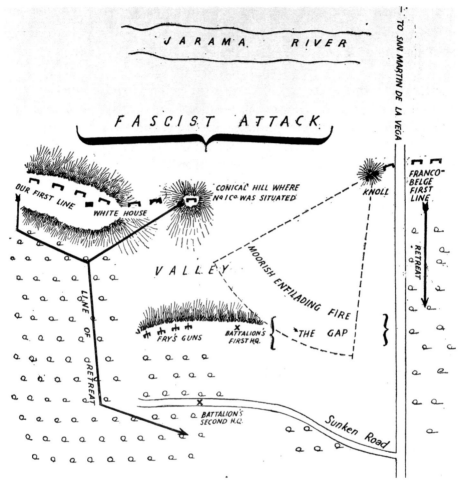

International Brigade and Fascist positions, Battle of Jarama, 1937.
(Map by Alexander Anderson, from *Records of the XV International Brigade*)

as if they were a set of medals. This physical testament to the savagery of war frightened me (his commentary on how dumdum bullets explode in the flesh was graphic), but at the same time this showed me that my hero-dad had put his life on the line for his convictions. A stranger once lobbed a verbal salvo at me: 'Your dad's a dirty communist,' he sneered. 'No he's not, he's a clean one,' I retorted.

What I secretly yearned for was a dad who was at home more, who spent time with me, who had a job that paid (instead of being a Communist Party organiser); I wanted a mum who didn't have to work, and who would not have to farm me out to my granny and aunties.

On that fateful day of 13 February 1937, the trenches of Harry Fry's Machine Gun Company were penetrated:

> Their uniforms were not unlike those of Spanish loyalist units, and when they drew near to our positions and displayed clenched-fist salutes, our company hesitated about whether or not to fire. Dr Hugh Thomas has got it wrong when he says it was the Moroccans who fooled us by singing 'The Internationale'.

Before being handed over to the Moors, his group of prisoners were compelled to witness several executions.

> The method of execution was for the firing party to present its rifles very close to the prisoners' heads, blowing their skulls to pieces. To my dying day I will recall how the blood shot up from their heads – but even more I will think of how Ted Dickenson lifted his clenched fist in the anti-fascist salute and called out in his last words 'Salud comrades.'
>
> We were marched down the valley under fire from our own lines, which killed more of our boys. Our wrists were tied with wire. The Moroccans kept us moving with whips and rifle-butts. Then we were bundled into lorries and driven under heavy guard to Navalcarnero, south of Brunete. Here we were herded into a pre-war prison, in filthy conditions. I encountered lice for the first time in my life there, which was no joke since my wound was untreated and they ate their way into it. We had no medical attention and were on starvation rations. What was more, we had to endure visits from some Italian fascist officers who came to taunt us. Sometimes, for the amusement of their senoritas who came with them, they would turn our Moroccan guards loose on us with boots, rifle-butts, etc. There is one thing I must stress, though, nobody ever gave away the fact I had been a Commissar to a Company, or I doubt if I would be sitting here talking to you now.

They were held at Navalcarnero for about two or three weeks.

A clear sense of time is something hard to keep hold of in these circumstances – but we were moved again, to Talavera de la Reina, further north and on the Tagus river. Our prison was a disused pottery warehouse, and we were held in conditions of great overcrowding with many Spanish anti-fascists arrested in the area after the town had fallen to Franco's troops.

International Brigade prisoners were tried by court-martial, without representation or having the charges translated.

We subsequently found out that the charges included military rebellion (ironical, when it was a military rebellion by Franco and the Falangists against a legally elected government which had brought most of us to Spain in the first place). In most cases they were sentenced to death or very long terms of imprisonment, varying from 30 years to solitary confinement for life. In any case, the random executions carried out at Talavera de la Reina made these sentences soon seem unimportant. One of the fatigues to which we were assigned was the enlarging of a mass grave for those executed in Talavera at this time, and on more than one occasion we had to watch prisoners engaged in this work being shot down by our guards and their bodies being thrown into this burial pit. I was on a working party whose orders were to cover up this mass grave after each batch of executions had been carried out, usually first thing in the morning...

One incident here stays clear in my mind. A soldier from the town itself, or nearby, had been conscripted into the Nationalist army but had deserted with the intention, we were told in prison, of reaching the Republican lines. Anyway, he was caught, and the local Falangists army unit decided to make this a spectacle for the townspeople and for our benefit too. The troops were turned out on parade, an army band played, and he was marched through the streets with hands bound – he was no more than a boy – to be shot.

Soon after this, most of the prisoners were transported by train to a prison in Salamanca.

It will be a long time yet before I forget the generosity of the

Spaniards who were our fellow prisoners there, many of whom, as we were soon to know, were destined for firing-squads. They were allowed to receive limited amounts of money from families and friends outside with which they could purchase some food, tobacco, and a little wine from the prison stores. For obvious reasons, we, as volunteers from abroad couldn't do this, but we didn't go without because the Spaniards regularly took collections from among themselves to buy from the store for us. By this time, moves were afoot for the first exchanges of prisoners between the two sides. We were in Salamanca for two months until the necessary negotiations were completed, and this brought about my repatriation to Britain, via France.

Willy Maley directed my attention to an account of these events held in the Moscow Archives of the Spanish Civil War, from a fellow member of the Machine Gun Battalion of the 15th Brigade, Tommy Bloomfield, who was interviewed after his release, on 5 February 1938. This 'debrief' (recounted in the third-person) records that Tommy believed the troops who overran their position to have been reinforcements.

Their task was to protect the other 15th Brigade companies behind them from sudden attacks, since the Brigade companies were busy with the expansion of positions. In this section there were also deputy officers, Battalion Commander, Captain Fry, the Political Commissar of No. 2 Company Donald Renton, and Ted Dickenson.

In addition to their usual infantry armament, they had four machine guns. Battalion Commander Captain Wintringham came in the morning and instructed them to hold this position at all costs. Captain Wintringham was wounded in the position on this occasion. Comrade Bloomfield, the company observer at the time, was always close to the officers, and is therefore well informed about the instructions given by the Battalion commander.

The fascist positions were about 400 yards away. The area between them and the fascists was very confusing. Hills, ditches and other bumps. In the afternoon around 3 o'clock a very violent artillery bombardment started, which continued until about 5 o'clock. Captain Fry sent a comrade back to inform the Battalion staff that a stronger attack by the fascists after the bombing was likely. During this artillery bombardment the Section had no losses. Following the artillery bombardment, the fascists' storm immediately set in on the trench. Bloomfield thinks he can remember that about 1,000 Spanish Falangists headed for the ditch. He remembers that the discipline and mood of his section was very good. Captain Fry felt that the position could not be maintained and was preparing to withdraw the section from the position at dawn and move further back. In preparation for this project, he left half an hour after the start of the fascist storm. So after the fascists' storm, four comrades with two machine guns go back. The section therefore only had two machine guns with it, one of which had already become incapable of fighting during the artillery bombardment. The rushing fascists made slow progress, but due to the confusing terrain, they had many opportunities to attack. When about an hour had passed, soldiers suddenly appeared in the back of the section, shouting 'Salud, comrades!' Since [the battalion] knew that Captain Fry had previously sent a reporter to the battalion staff, they believed that it was a Spanish formation sent for reinforcement. Suddenly, however, they were ambushed.

It took only ten minutes to march the captives behind enemy lines. On this short journey, three of the POWs met their deaths at the hands of their escorts. Their names are set out in the report:

Comrade Philip Ellis [Elias], Englishman. The latter asked one of the Spanish guards whether he was allowed to smoke, which was allowed to him by the fascist. When he reached into his pocket to take out a cigarette, he was shot by the same fascist.
    Comrade T Stevens, English. Stevens was killed by the same bullet as comrade Ellis, since the bullet went through Ellis and then killed comrade Stevens behind him.
Ted Dickenson, English. The shooting of this comrade took place in the following way: the moment he was captured, Dickenson had jumped at the comrade Fry, who had just been wounded on the right arm, and was able to tear off his officer's braids and other badges in good time. However, Dickenson lost the time to remove

his own galons himself, so he was captured as an officer.

During Don's time as a prisoner, the only reading matter available in English was the bible. He read it twice from beginning to end, which only served to consolidate his view that religion was the opium of the people. Unlike some other International Brigade volunteers, Don did not go back to Spain after repatriation. As he explains in Ian MacDougall's *Voices from the Spanish Civil War*, 'a decision had been taken' that he should be 'in charge of anti-fascist work in the East End of London and particularly among the unemployed where Mosley was making some inroads'.

***

As NUWM organiser in the East End of London until the outbreak of the Second World War, he planned numerous direct actions, using tactics more recently associated with Trident Ploughshares, Pollok Free State and Extinction Rebellion. He devised and mounted a series of stunts that succeeded in grabbing mainstream press attention. It wasn't often that he talked to me about politics (much as I wished he would) but when he did, it was the 1930s he returned to.

I remember him telling me about an occasion which necessitated seeking out the thinnest member of the Unemployed Workers' Movement (this was a strongly contested role); and also the fattest (there were very few contenders in this category). From the fat man Don acquired an overcoat. Early on the morning of Hogmanay 1938, a long banner proclaiming 'For a Happy New Year the Unemployed Must not Starve in 1939' was wrapped round and round the skinny volunteer. After the banner was concealed under the capacious overcoat, my dad and this 'portly' man made their way to the London Monument at the north end of London Bridge. As soon as they had determined there were no other visitors, they rammed a wedge under the entrance door. At the top of the 311 steps they went out onto the observation platform, where the banner was unwound over the side:

Our banner hung over the City of London and employees of the surrounding business houses gazed up at it with varying degrees of amazement and sympathy.'

NUWM demonstrations and marches were taking place all over Britain. In 1938 Scottish Hunger marchers were pictured at a soup kitchen in Waverley Market, Edinburgh.

They must have escaped arrest (or possibly Don left the other man at the foot of the monument). At any rate, that same day, he wired an unemployed ecclesiastical carver:

That telegram read: 'Buy plywood – make coffin, funeral tonight.' Side by side with this I sent messages out to all the National Unemployed Workers' Movement branches in London asking them to rally to attend a funeral. Our coffin turned up in Piccadilly Circus as large as life! On its sides was written: 'He Did Not Get Winter Relief'. Great crowds of holidaymakers thronged the streets. They had no idea this was a stunt, but the poignant message of the coffin

On 1 February 1939 the *News Chronicle* pictured a scuffle with the police under the headline
'Workless Take Their Coffin to Parliament'.

struck home; they raised their hats in silent sympathy, and many became
allies of the unemployed in their fight for work or full maintenance.

Don wrote a regular *Tribune* column after returning from Spain. In 1939,
under the headline 'Starvation Was Not News Till We Made It News', he
tells the story of more of these demonstrations, including occupations of
Unemployed Assistance Board offices at Limehouse, Islington and Lewisham:

Officials were frantically pounding at the doors of the waiting
rooms with sledgehammers.
   Behind those doors were unemployed men grimly determined
to hold possession of the rooms until the Board decided to grant
Winter Relief to every unemployed man and woman. It was
November 16, 1938 – the unemployed stay-in strikes had begun.
Only when the police smashed their way in with heavy hammers
and crowbars, were the strikers finally ejected – but not before

truncheons had been drawn. The demands made by the National Unemployed Workers' Movement for Winter Relief payments of 2/6d for each adult, with 1/- for each dependent child, for the first time struck the headlines.

In a confidential circular issued to Area Offices of the Unemployment Assistance Board, Ernest Brown, Minister of Labour, contemptuously referred to the stay-in strikes as 'inefficiently organised'. But their effect has been seen in the removal, by officials, of the doors from the waiting rooms in many of the most important Unemployment Board Offices, including those at Thames House, headquarters of the Board.

Another action that succeeded in attracting mainstream press coverage was the 'lie-down' in Oxford Street on 20 December 1938. Don writes:

Demanding Winter Relief, Trafalgar Square, London, reported in the *Daily Worker* on 7 February 1939.

Snow lay thickly in Oxford Street. Churned to filthy slush by heavy traffic, it did not dissuade us; hunger bites more deeply because of the cold. Lying in the road before onrushing traffic, with posters over our bodies proclaiming the demand for 'Work and Bread', we were warmed by the sympathy of thousands of shoppers who refused to assist the police to move us.

On 23 December, under the headline 'Jobless Invade a Hotel – London Police Called as Fifty Fail to Get Tea Served', the front page of the *New York Times* reported that

about 50 members of an unemployed workers' movement, including three women, walked into the Grill Room of the Ritz Hotel in Piccadilly today, and asked to have tea served.

But as Don recounts with a rather different perspective in his *Tribune* column:

Then came our visit to the Ritz – for tea? – NO! – to expose our lack of food and the treatment received by us at the hands of the kind of people who can afford to frequent the Ritz, and who make no mistakes about their way to the Tea Lounge. The manager was perturbed – not at our empty bellies, which he could have filled as an example to Ernest Brown, but by the fact that I wore my hat while inside the Grill Room.

'Workless Invade the Ritz', screamed the newspaper placards – while in the House of Commons, Ernest Brown was refusing to agree to the Labour suggestion that Winter Relief payments and Christmas grants should at once be made to the unemployed.

As mentioned earlier, Don was incensed at Julian Symons' characterisation of the activities of the NUWM as 'nothing more than well-organised stunts' and 'cynically effective farce'. The *Edinburgh Evening News* published his letter of rebuttal in 1960:

Having served in the International Brigade in Spain, and in the leadership of the activities of the National Unemployed Workers' Movement, I wish to challenge Julian Symons' interpretation of what took place in the hungry winter of 1938.

I was the person responsible for convening the lie-down strike in London's Oxford Circus. Over 100 men and women were involved, in contrast to his conception of 40. They held up the traffic for a much longer period than he states. As they were lifted off the street by policemen, who were unable to obtain reinforcements because of the traffic jam, they went back and resumed their position on the road. Wal Hannington's book *Black Coffins and the Unemployed* contains a much more accurate description of what took place than that of which Symons gives.

It amuses me to read what Symons says took place when the unemployed invaded the Ritz Hotel in London. The unemployed did not take a wrong turning. They were led there by me, and led directly into the Grill Room, where I addressed them, the assembled waiters, the manager, and the police from the platform usually occupied by the orchestra...

True, we produced coppers for tea; that had also been planned – and planned to take place in the Ritz Grill Room. We knew what they usually purveyed: but what we wanted to do was to contrast the terrible poverty of the unemployed with the standard of living enjoyed by the frequenters of the Ritz Hotel. I am probably the first Socialist who ever addressed a meeting in these surroundings and circumstances.

Following his return to London from Spain and up until the outbreak of the Second World War, Don spoke at hundreds of meetings in support of the Republic and against the British Union of Fascists.

* * *

The submarine *Thetis* sank 160ft to the bottom of Liverpool Bay on 1 June 1939. Only four members of crew survived; the other 99 died from suffocation or drowning. In the hope of increasing the safety of submarine crews, on 18 July Don and three International Brigade comrades – George Ives, Paddy Duff and Bill Alexander – took part in a 'self-experiment' devised by Professor JBS Haldane. For these men, political activism at home was on a continuum with confronting fascism in Spain. I see their personal courage as evidence of the

Reporting the *Thetis* experiment in Don Renton's *Tribune* column, 28 July 1939.,

spirit of social altruism which underpinned their politics. Haldane's findings were presented to the *Thetis* Inquiry and the participants in his experiment were commended by the Judge 'for their fortitude in seeking to devise the best means of providing safety for the men of the submarine service'.

A left-wing biologist and supporter of the Spanish Republic, Haldane had no problem with the idea that news of their courage might serve as an antidote to the venom with which leftist activists were often treated. The view of a Lady Winterton that 'It is a pity that men who come home unemployed and make a nuisance of themselves with coffins by chaining themselves to railings were not shot in Spain' is prominently presented in a box at the head of Don's *Tribune* column for 28 July 1939, alongside a photograph of the five men shortly after emerging from the experiment. The volunteers are identified as:

> BILL ALEXANDER: Englishman. Joined British Battalion in Spain in the early days of the war. Recommended to be decorated for bravery on the field. Promoted to the rank of lieutenant.
> DON RENTON: Scotsman. Joined British Battalion December, 1936. Held rank of Political Commissar in No. 2 Company. Wounded and taken prisoner while defending Madrid at the battle of Jarama. Now London organiser of the National Unemployed Workers' Movement.
> PROFESSOR HALDANE: Professor of Biometry, London University,

author of numerous scientific papers on human chemical physiology. Went to Spain to find out all about air raids and wrote his famous book *A.R.P.* on the basis on his observations of actual conditions there. Big, endlessly active, genial, known affectionately to all the International Brigade as 'The Professor'.

PADDY DUFF: Irishman. Joined British Battalion of the International Brigade September 1936. Took part in every major action in which the Battalion was involved. Wounded five times. Finally disabled by gunshot wounds in the battle on the Ebro. Now in London for operations to restore him physically.

GEORGE IVES: Englishman. Served in the anti-tank section of the International Brigade. Taken prisoner by Fascists. Experienced nine months' imprisonment in the San Pedro concentration camp near Burgos. Finally exchanged for Fascist prisoners held by the government.

They had met 'The Professor' in Madrigueras, where he advised troops on how to survive a poison gas attack. They had probably also met his wife, Charlotte Haldane in Paris, where they would have stopped before travelling by train to Perpignan on the Spanish border. My uncle, Bill Cranston, interviewed by Iain MacDougall, recalls Charlotte Haldane's bracingly direct advice on avoiding venereal disease, by abstention, in the brothel where he overnighted in Paris.

Posing the question, 'Why were the men on the *Thetis* unable to use the Davis apparatus to escape from their tomb of steel?', Don explains:

> Professor Haldane's theory was that the men found dead in the escape hatch vomited violently on donning the Davis apparatus. Their lungs were unable to stand the effect of pure oxygen after prolonged carbon-dioxide poisoning. Professor Haldane considered it probable that in this condition they tore the Davis apparatus from their faces and as a result were drowned in the hatch through which they had hoped to reach safety.

Haldane had already used himself as a human guinea pig, remaining in an airtight chamber for around 14 hours, before testing his provisional conclusions through the participation of the former IB men.

Inside the circular chamber in which the test was made were three cylinders containing nitrogen, carbon dioxide and air, and instruments to measure atmospheric pressure and the carbon dioxide content of the atmosphere. Those inside were observed through a small plate glass window. Before they entered, George Ives was designated to be in charge of the phone link to the outside world and Bill Alexander to act as Haldane's clerk. Don writes:

We entered the Chamber at 2.40pm on Tuesday, July 18. Behind us the heavy doors were swung shut. This completely excluded the entry of good air. George took his place beside the phone, which promptly broke down. Our language at this point helped to vitiate the atmosphere. Fortunately contact with the outside was established in a few minutes.

Don Renton at the time of volunteering as a human guinea pig for Professor Haldane's experiments on the effects of pressure on humans.

Paddy, Bill and I sat down close to the steel door of the inner chamber, hardly daring to move in case we should upset some of the apparatus. Professor Haldane remained on his feet checking up every detail. His height was a nuisance to him. We found time to be amused as he slanged the pipes which crossed the ceiling.

The nitrogen was turned on. The purpose of this was to reduce the oxygen content. As it hissed into the chamber we experienced a curious sensation in our ears. When we blew our noses our ear drums pained. It did not affect our breathing. With this point reached, the nitrogen was turned off. Next came the carbon dioxide. This was used from the cylinder to save time. Without the use of these artificial methods it would have been necessary to stay in the chamber until such time as our own breathing produced the gas which had suffocated the crew.

By 3pm we were panting heavily. Our lungs were wheezing like broken-down bagpipes as our chests rose and fell. Normal breathing averages 10 to 20 inhalations a minute. At this stage our laboured lungs were reaching 40 to 50. We were fully occupied with the effort of breathing... Five minutes later we were perspiring fiercely, although our jackets, pullovers and other heavy clothing had been left outside. The heat was mounting rapidly. It soon became almost unbearable. It was probably cooler in the *Thetis*.

Condensed breath rolled in beads of water down the walls of the chamber. As condensation developed it became increasingly difficult for Professor Haldane to read the gauge of the thermometer and to study the other instruments. The strain on mental capacity was shown by the fact that Bill found it difficult to take down a number of figures. Elementary calculations were soon beyond him. Paddy was holding his head in his hands and complaining about a headache. In a light-headed manner I began to compare the atmosphere with that in the Morden Tube. George was not so badly affected. Our own breathing was rapidly increasing the carbon dioxide in the chamber. Professor Haldane estimated that the rapidity of this process was several times greater than in the *Thetis* because of the much smaller space occupied by us.

At 3.30pm, Haldane released some pure air from the third cylinder, warning that this would ease their breathing for a short time only. As 4.00pm approached, Don recounts:

Paddy was in a really bad state by this time. Bill and I were in no better fettle. The effect on Professor Haldane and George Ives was a little less pronounced. To eliminate the risk of serious illness for any one of us, Professor Haldane decided to prepare for evacuating the chamber. This decision was communicated to the outside by George Ives and in the last few minutes the professor took a sample of air for further analysis outside the chamber to supplement those he had made within.

As soon as the chamber doors were opened from the outside, they escaped its confines into the clean atmosphere. Davis decompression apparatus was available for immediate use.

George Ives, Paddy and I managed to don it without assistance. Bill Alexander made an effort to do so but was at once violently sick. Within half a minute of leaving, Paddy and I were undergoing terrible torment with the worst headaches we had ever experienced. Nevertheless, we managed to keep the apparatus on for five minutes. George Ives, who had been least affected in the chamber, developed a headache after he had removed the Davis apparatus, which he had worn for five minutes. Professor Haldane stood outside the chamber during this time, breathing ordinary air and observing our reactions.

Haldane later told the *Thetis* Inquiry that the group were within two hours of the time when the weakest of them would have died. 'There is no doubt in our minds about how the men in the escape hatch of the *Thetis* must have felt,' Don writes, closing with the conclusions to be drawn from the experiment:

Davis apparatus must be used before the atmosphere of the submarine becomes too thick.

It should be used some time before the men enter the escape hatch so that they can accustom themselves to the oxygen, thus eliminating the risk of vomiting in the escape hatch, where if the apparatus is removed the wearer will be drowned.

Submarines should carry sufficient supplies of soda-lime to absorb the carbon dioxide and thus increase the chance of escape for the crew if the submarine becomes involved in a disaster.

It would have been important to Don to supply this factual data in such detail. He was a great believer in the power of education and human ingenuity, and he had a real interest in scientific developments.

* * *

Daily Worker staff c 1939. Queenie Renton third left.

The story of how my parents met is very romantic: strangers on a boat going down the River Thames, falling in love at first sight. They married at Stepney register office in 1939, and so most likely crossed paths after Don's return from Spain. Quite what they were both doing on that boat, I'll never know.

Their backgrounds couldn't have been more different. Queenie was from a Jewish family and her liaison with a firebrand lefty was not well received. She told me her father had considered sitting shiva (a traditional mourning ritual) for her, because she 'married out'. I never learned any details of her early married life in London, although I do have a photograph of the staff of the *Daily Worker* from the late 1930s – and there is my mum, peeking out from a phalanx of resolute men; her beautiful face framed in a cloud of tight black curls; her shy, almond eyes. She looked very like the film actress and inventor, Hedy Lamarr.

Very occasionally, Queenie talked to me about her young days. As a teenager, she adored Shakespeare, learning all her favourite passages off by heart, something she encouraged me to do. She practised piano four hours a day in hopes of becoming a professional musician, a career which never materialised. She could play by ear and could play from memory Beethoven,

Tchaikovsky and Chopin. She had been very close to her father and loved their evening walks together, the aroma of roasting chestnuts in the London fog, stopping at a glowing brazier to buy a pennyworth – if she had a guilty pang at having skimped piano practice, she would try to force the thought away, convinced that he could read her mind. She spun me a tale of London as a loved and magical place, the river running through it a living, mythic entity.

After Queenie died of a heart attack in 1967, when I was 17 – a shattering event that threw my life off kilter – these fragments became talismanic, a precious cargo of passed-down memories. In the course of researching this chapter, disconcertingly, some have shimmered into mirage.

At the end of the Second World War, in which he served in the Royal Artillery and took part in the anti-aircraft defence of London and other targets of the Blitz, Don returned to Scotland and a post as full-time secretary of the Communist Party for the Lothians area. As far as I know, Queenie, a shorthand typist, brought in the only wage.

In the early '50s, the Communist party bought us a one-bedroom, top-floor flat in Meadowbank, overlooking St Margaret's shunting yard and with views to the River Forth and Fife beyond. I remember my excitement, aged three or four, as a squad of comrades scraped off the Victorian varnished wallpaper; one of them stripped the doors with a tool that looked like a dragon spitting flame; another man painted them, deftly simulating wood grain.

We had hardly any furniture. In the front room there was a dark brown settee, two armchairs, a piano and a piano stool. Our neighbours used to come out onto the landings to listen to my mum playing the piano. On the odd occasion we had visitors, my dad would glow with pride and ask her to play 'Greensleeves'. I haven't inherited her gift, but her music is in my bones.

There was an old cast-iron range in the kitchen which was sometimes painted with black lead and the stainless-steel trim sandpapered until it shone. One of my loveliest childhood times was when my mum took me on her knee and 'told stories in the fire'. I would stare through the bars of the fire basket into a glowing miniature landscape whose contours changed as the coal burned, creating caves and mountains and chasms. I was convinced I could see Brer Rabbit and Alice in this fiery wonderland. (When I was about seven, the boiler at the back of the range broke. It was never mended, so that was the end of hot running water.)

* * *

Until I was ten, I spent weeks at a time with my granny, Julia, and with Don's sisters, Isa and Nancy, who looked after me as if I was one of their own. Isa and Nancy both lived in the mining village of Newcraighall, on the road from Edinburgh to Musselburgh, their husbands Bill Cranston and Andrew King working at the Klondyke pit. Isa moved to Niddrie when I was very small, but Nancy lived in Newcraighall until I was eight, and so a lot of my happiest early childhood memories are of being there, playing with my cousins Julia and Billy. One thing that irked me was that everyone around me spoke Scots, but I was told off if I did (as Isa put it: '*I* say aye. *You* say yes.'). I can only imagine that this notion of 'proper' speech was something my mum wanted, because it wasn't remotely my aunties' style.

The cottages at Newcraighall were on an identical pattern used for miners' rows throughout Scotland, one two-roomed dwelling above and one below. Nancy's was on the ground floor. You went straight into a scullery, where there was a sink with a cold-water tap, a stove and a small cupboard. A boxed-off area accommodated the inside lavvy. A smelly bar of carbolic soap kept at the back of the sink was used for washing everything and everyone. Through a door was the living room, where the fire was kept going, night

Out to play in Newcraighall, 1954. Julia King (centre) Jennie Renton (second right).

and day. Nancy and Andrew slept here on a bed settee. A door on the back wall led 'ben the hoose', where we children slept, Billy at one end of the bed, me and Julia at the other. To keep us warm in winter in those impoverished pre-duvet days, heavy coats were piled on top of us.

I remember Billy telling me to stop waking him up in the night shouting for my 'ma'. When I was about four, I threw a huge tantrum as my mum tried to get me on a bus to my auntie's before going on to work. I lay on the pavement and pounded the tarmac with my heels, screaming my head off and feeling she would surely have to give in. But what ensued was a quiet conversation between her and Nancy, and after that I was farmed out for weeks on end.

But I did love Newcraighall – playing on the chute and swings at the park with Julia, going for a penny jubilee at the tiny odoriferous provisions store, watching a man skin a hare at his open front door, delving with sticks in clogged syvers. Sometimes Julia and I would walk all the way to Portobello along lanes cutting through farmland fringed with poppies and brambles. The atmosphere of the village is captured in Bill Douglas's film trilogy about his childhood.

During school holidays we were put outside to play, come rain or shine, and for our dinner in the middle of the day we got jam pieces handed out of the window. I complained that Billy was getting four slices, while Julia and I only got two. As Billy was two years older than me and Julia two years younger, I reckoned I should get three slices. I was told that Billy was a boy, and that was that. I remember one Gala Day being crestfallen that, because my dad wasn't a miner, I wasn't allowed to join the children's fancy dress procession. With three coloured circles pinned to my front, meant to be traffic lights, I watched from the pavement, envious of my cousin Julia with pots and pans tied to a pinny and the slogan 'The way to a man's heart is through his stomach'.

In the '50s – incidentally, a repressive decade where child abuse was commonplace – there was conventionally a sharp divide between what working-class men and women did. The women of my family organised childcare among themselves and it should be underlined that it was the support of Don's wife, sisters and mother that made it possible for him to continue to concentrate full time on his politics after he became a father.

* * *

After leaving the CP, Don was in a political wilderness for several years and in 1958 he was one of the many left-wingers and politicians from around the world to be courted by Moral Re-Armament, an outfit ostensibly dedicated to change starting with the individual. It grew out of Frank Buchman's Oxford Movement and now goes under the name Initiatives of Change. The MP for Edinburgh Central, Tom Oswald, paid for us to visit the extremely grand MRA centre in Caux, Switzerland. It seems quite out of character that Don accepted this invitation – I have no idea what his thinking was. Certainly, he never joined MRA. Perhaps he just wanted to get close to this particular ideological enemy for observation purposes.

After a few years out of the CP, his application to join the Labour Party was accepted and he became councillor for Craigmillar in 1962, holding the seat until 1968, when it was won by the SNP.

When I was ten, in 1960, I asked if I could just come straight home from school and became a 'latch-key kid'. It was around this time that I picked up a *Weekly News* and read an illustrated report about the Nazi death factories. My world changed right there. I thought, *That would have been my mum, because she's Jewish.* Then I thought, *It would have been my dad too, because of his politics.* Flooded with dread, I then realised that, *Even if I had been a wee baby, it would have been me too.* As I grew older, I had the even grimmer realisation that the capacity for violence is not confined to any particular social or ethnic group. It seems to be a universal potential that can be triggered even in the most peaceable of folk.

Our home life in the 1960s was turbulent. My parents argued, mainly over Don's drinking. Queenie would make an evening meal. Sometimes he arrived at teatime, more often after the pubs closed at ten. Up to high doh, her eyes would bulge with anxiety as his key turned in the lock – I became quite an expert in interpreting the degree of inebriation the sound expressed. On Sundays, when the pubs were all shut, there were reconciliations and promises that were kept about as well as when he signed the Band of Hope abstinence pledge aged 14.

The state of our flat was chaotic. Some of my friends were forbidden to return because they went home so manky. The atmosphere of constant stress started making me come out in hives, which I would plaster with Caladryl lotion. With no running hot water, my sketchy efforts in personal cleanliness failed to eliminate its orange residue on my neck. In my first year at Leith Academy Secondary, I was publicly upbraided by a teacher who said my bedraggled appearance let the school down and ordered me to adorn my hair with kirby grips requisitioned from a tidy classmate. The humiliation went deep.

Looking back, I can see that Queenie felt depressed and defeated during this time, and that the way she poured her heart out to me was a heavy load to bear for a youngster, although there was also something heady in being let in on all this adult stuff. There were no real boundaries to what she shared. I always took her side, without any insight into what Don himself might be going through. Sometimes she would bang out a piece by Tchaikovsky on the piano, then crash down the lid and hold up her puffy fingers, sobbing that those Imperial typewriters had ruined her hands. After she died, I held my father's drinking and absences responsible and we later fell out badly. I'm relieved to say that we made it up when I was in my early 20s.

The underlying reality was that I blamed myself, not my dad, but this was too unbearable to face. Queenie had been getting breathless climbing the stair and of course, Don had no idea – by that time, they never climbed the stair together. One day in November 1967 she had gone to the doctor and he referred her to a consultant. She tore up her letter of referral right in front of me, saying that they would only tell her to move to a ground floor and she would never manage to do that. A couple of weeks later, she collapsed outside our stair door after I'd gone to school. By the time an ambulance arrived about half an hour later, she was dead on the pavement.

I went to stay with a school friend and after a while, Don went to live with Bill and Isa Cranston in Niddrie.

In May 1972, Don was elected councillor for Sighthill. For a brief time he was a bailie but I know he was uncomfortable in that role. Even before the fancy streetlight to mark the residence of a city bailie could be erected, he resigned – on the basis that the proposed expenditure on Commonwealth Games facilities should be spent on social housing, a perennial campaign focus throughout his life.

When Don died in 1977, hundreds of people turned out for his 'red' funeral. His coffin was draped with the banner of the International Brigade. The speakers were Mick McGahey, Tom Murray and Councillor Jimmy Kerr (Don was proud of the fact he had encouraged Mick McGahey to join the Young Communist League). In the days before his death, he had been visited by a series of friends and comrades whose final words of farewell was invariably 'No pasaran!'.

Ten years later, Edinburgh District Council named redeveloped housing in Wauchope Terrace 'Renton House'. Marking the occasion, Craigmillar Festival commented:

> During his time in Craigmillar, Donald played a very active part in the early years of the Craigmillar Festival Society, becoming its co-chair in the late 1960s. Naming the sheltered housing after Donald Renton is a fine tribute to a man of immense bravery with an uncommon conviction in pursuance of improving the lot of others. It is a tribute that will be welcomed by many local residents who have good reason to be thankful that they had a councillor of Donald Renton's stature serving their interests in the council chamber.

Don had a smile that would light up a room, a palpable decency and will to make a difference in the world. He sought to promote justice and adopted an international perspective. Although drink was a weakness, he was never a threatening man. There was an honesty and idealism about him which remain inspiring to me. He was a convinced revolutionary and an inveterate Marxist-Leninist propagandist, who would have concurred with the view of French Jacobin Nicholas Chamfort, that revolutions are not made with rosewater. Don was never one to flinch from fighting – literally – for what he believed in.

* * *

History, like personal memory, is a collage of fragments. During the course of writing this piece, various pertinent documents have come, unexpectedly, into my hands. As well as Owen Dudley Edwards alerting me to Don's *Tribune* columns, William Lytle of Edinburgh Books just a few doors down from my own bookshop in the West Port came in to tell me of something that might interest me that had just come into stock: *Records of the 15th Brigade*. I could not resist buying this copy, the title emblazoned in gold on the red cover, the fragile remnant of the dustwrapper preserved between pages along with handwritten notes identifying Scots who appear in its grainy photographic illustrations. An inscription dated 1 July 1939 from 'A. Donaldson' (likely to be the Coatbridge volunteer Alexander James Donaldson), reads:

A mi compañero Andrew McLerie con algunos recueros inolvidables. (To my comrade Andrew McLerie with some unforgettable memories). The Acknowledgements mention an Alex Donaldson as being among those who compiled the publication of 308 pages, remarkably brought from conception to print in under a month – guerilla publishing, if ever there was!

Although Don is not mentioned in its pages, I find something intensely evocative about this direct, material link with the Madrid of 1938 and it has served as a talisman while writing this memoir.

I have also been very interested to come across Julius Ruiz's *The 'Red Terror' and the Spanish Civil War: Revolutionary Violence in Madrid*. Ruiz, who teaches at the

Records of the XV Brigade published by the Commissariat of War XV Brigade. Madrid, 1938.
(Cover design: Alexander Anderson)

University of Edinburgh, has forebears who fought on both sides of the conflict. His focus in this book is the execution of around 50,000 people by Republican sympathisers in Madrid in summer 1936, just as the war was starting. He fulfils his commitment to seek objectivity in a context of partisan historiography.

At one point, he gives a harrowing account of scenes of panic in the aftermath of Franco's victory, when hundreds of Republicans flocked to the beach at Alicante in expectation of being evacuated by French ships. But Franco's navy blocked entry to the rescue vessels. When it became clear that there would be no escape by sea, it is reported that terror swept the crowd, some of them committing suicide on the spot, by knife or bullet.

Personally, I try to hold on to the belief that it is possible to be a pacifist. Untested, this has to be a position that, in extremis, may prove no more than a comforting delusion. And at the same time, I believe that I would not be alive today if people had not taken up arms against fascism.

My dad's heroism is something I deeply respect. And that heroism was by no means confined to the field of battle. But as an off-and-on attender of Quaker meetings, I am reluctant to contribute to any heroic-soldier narrative. And then there is the hard-line certainty of his Marxist-Leninism; whereas at heart, I am more like my mum – accepting, even embracing, uncertainty.

In the light of these contradictions, how much am I my father's daughter?

Perhaps a clue lies in where I cast my vote. In recent elections, I was among a few hundred people who voted for an offbeat candidate who styles himself 'Bonnie Prince Bob'. A far cry from the other 'Bonnie Prince', Bonnie Prince Bob has a satiric sense of humour.

More importantly, his manifesto supports universal basic income; social housing for all who require it; education and health systems funded solely by public capital; abolition of the monarchy; and reclaiming its land for the Scottish people.

Who does that remind me of?

3

GEORDIE WATTERS

'I'm away to Spain to fight the fascists. Who will join me?'

Tam Watters

MY FATHER, GEORGE WATTERS (always known as Geordie), was born on 26 September 1904. The family home was at West Seaside in Prestonpans. His father, George Dunn Watters, born in 1867, was a miner who fought in the First World War. George D Watters and his wife Isabella had a family of six sons and three daughters – their first child was born in 1890 and their last in 1909. Life would have been very hard for Isabella. George D Watters' military pension card shows that in October 1917 he still had four dependent children at home, including Geordie. The few shillings a week from that pension would not have gone far. One of Geordie's four older brothers, Dave, also fought in the First World War. Most of the siblings lived to a very old age, some to almost 100, but Dave and Geordie both suffered ill health and did not enjoy such long lives. Dave had suffered gas poisoning during the war and Geordie's health suffered from the horrific treatment inflicted on him in the Spanish jails. The fact that both men worked in the coal mines no doubt contributed significantly to their health problems in later years.

Geordie and his brothers had staunch socialist principles and I have often wondered what made them so passionate in their political beliefs. Part of the reason might have been that they were all miners, living in extremely poor mining communities where everyone was struggling to survive the daily toils of that environment. Any improvements in their terms and conditions of employment would be gained only after a hard fight.

Accidents and deaths were commonplace in the mines, and many families were affected by them. George D Watters' nephew, William Watters, died at Prestongrange Colliery in 1902, crushed by a runaway hutch; he was only 14 years old.

Geordie told me he had first become politically active in 1922 at the age of 17. In 1923, he had ten dozen copies of *Workers Weekly* delivered to his home in Prestonpans for him to distribute every week. That was the official paper of the British Communist Party. It later became the *Daily Worker* and is now called the *Morning Star*. Later he became a regular reader of *Soviet Weekly*, which was first published in 1942.

Geordie and older brothers Dave and Robert joined the Communist Party during the early 1920s. I know Geordie and Dave remained members of the Party for the rest of their lives and I suspect Robert would have done so too.

During the General Strike of 1926 the miners, including Geordie, were on strike for six months, fighting a huge cut in wages and an increase in their working hours. Future Prime Minister, Winston Churchill, suggested bringing in the army to control the strikers. That reinforced Geordie's deep dislike of the Tories. Churchill wanted to arm the soldiers but the Prime Minister, Stanley Baldwin, opposed the idea, saying that if the soldiers were armed it would be unnecessarily antagonistic to the strikers and, if any striker were shot, it would cause even more problems. Even King George v had tried to defuse the situation by saying, 'Try living on their wages before you judge them.' It is difficult to believe that, in 2002, in a BBC television poll, the British public voted Churchill the greatest Briton of all time.

The miners worked very hard in dangerous, health-damaging conditions, only to be rewarded with barely enough to exist on. But even then, their lives were better than previous generations had been forced to tolerate.

A report by RF Franks to the Children's Employment Commission on the East of Scotland District was published in 1842, eight years after the abolition of slavery. Reading it, you have to ask, what was the life of these children, if not slavery?

'Tranent Colliery parish of Tranent –
(Messrs. William and H. F. Cadell).

No. 157. James Wood, 12 years old, coal-hewer:

I have worked below ground three years, except when I was laid idle
by a pick striking a piece of metal, which cast fire, and caused me the
loss of my eye. Was off idle near 12 months.

I go down at five in the morning, and come away about seven at
night; except when bad air is in the pit, when we are compelled to
stop away sometimes for three and four days together. A little tea,
which is made overnight, and pieces of bread, is all that we get to eat
till we return, when we have broth or some such. The part of the pit I
work in is very wet and I am obliged to sit on a bit of coal to keep the
water off.

Sometimes I change myself after work; do so when home early;
never on full long days.

Comment at end of note: Reads well and writes tolerably.

No. 158. James Neil aged 10 years, coal-hewer:

Been below 18 months; the work is gai sore. Place of work is not
very dry. Never got hurt, but the work has given me the piles, which
pain me when I sit. I work from four and five in the morning till six
and seven at night, and it fatigues me much. Sometimes I change my
clothes; not frequent, as it is so late.

*Comment at end of note: Can read and write a little; knows a little
Scripture history.*

No. 160. William Kerr, 11 years old, coal-bearer. Wrought below five
years. Goes down at five in morning, returns six and seven at night:

Gets my bread as other laddies do. Carries coal on my back. Can fill
a basket of 5cwt. in six journeys. It is 150 fathoms from my father's
room to pit bottom.

James and Anne Maley on their wedding day,
25 March 1949.

Archibald Campbell McAskill Williams as a child with
parents John and Julia.

Queenie and Donald Renton, 1939.

Ellen Watters with her three children in April
1937, when she feared Geordie might have
died in Spain. His image was added by the
photographer, showing him with the family.

1930s poster for the anarcho-syndicalist union
Confederación Nacional del Trabajo (CNT).
(Wikimedia Commons)

Propaganda poster of the Francoists, 1930s.
(Wikimedia Commons)

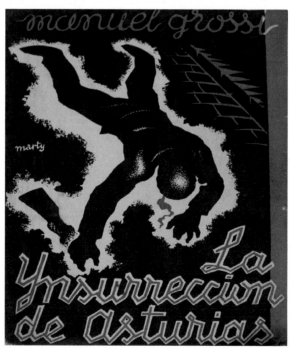

Pamphlet about the Asturias insurrection,
a prelude to the Spanish Civil War.

Work detail, imprisoned International Brigaders, 1937. (Alamy)

International Brigade POWs being handed cigarettes for a propaganda newsreel, March 1937.
The cigarettes were later confiscated. (British Pathé)

IB veterans Don Renton (left), Giovanni Pesce (centre) and Tom Murray (second right) at the gathering in Firenze in 1976 to mark the 40th anniversary of the formation of the International Brigade.

The medal awarded to veterans to mark the 40th anniversary of the formation of the International Brigade.

IB veteran Steve Fullarton (left) with Tam and Ishbel Watters (right), holding the banner of the Scottish contingent of the British Battalion of the International Brigade. (Photo: Angela Graham)

James Maley (left), Steve Fullarton (right) with the banner of the Scottish contingent of the British Battalion of the International Brigade on 11 October 2003 at the La Pasionaria statue, Clydeside.

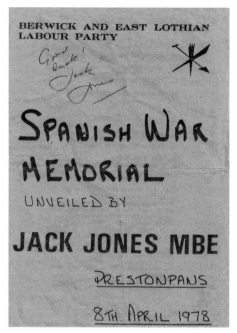

Leaflet signed by trade unionist Jack Jones (1913–2009), who served with the British Battalion of the XV International Brigade as Political Commissar of the Major Attlee Company.

Rebekah Lumsden as Ellen Watters in *549: Scots of the Spanish Civil War.*
(Photo: Mihaela Bodlovic)

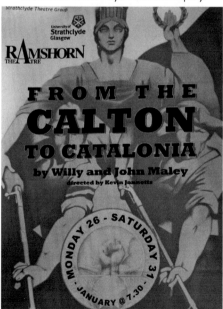

Poster for the Strathclyde Theatre Group production of *From the Calton to Catalonia* by Willy and John Maley at the Ramshorn Theatre 2009.

Poster featuring the Clydeside statue of La Pasionaria, for the 2016 Rutherglen Town Hall performance of *From the Calton to Catalonia* by Willy and John Maley.

Robbie Gordon as Geordie Watters in the Wonder Fools production of *549: Scots of the Spanish Civil War*. (Photo: Mihaela Bodlovic)

Dramatic combat scene from *549: Scots of the Spanish Civil War*. (Photo: Mihaela Bodlovic)

Stained-glass window in Prestonpans Labour Club honouring local International Brigaders Bill Dickson, Jock Gilmour, Jimmy Kempton and Geordie Watters.

Stained-glass window commemorating the International Brigades, City Hall, Belfast. Irish and Scottish volunteers fought side-by-side at Jarama. (Wikimedia Commons)

I am o'er sair gone at times, as the hours are so long and the work gai sair. Never have the opportunity to get some sleep.

Comment at end of note: Went to school once; reads very badly; has no scriptural knowledge whatever.

A law was passed in August 1842 – the Mines and Collieries Act – that stopped children under the age of ten and women from working underground in Britain. Children over the age of ten would have continued to endure barbaric conditions. Maybe the authorities should have been more concerned about the terrible lives these children had and less interested in how well they knew the bible.

World War One had just ended and life should have been getting back to normal when, in January 1919, tragedy again struck the Watters family. Oldest brother William was killed in a horrific accident at Prestongrange Colliery, where the brothers worked. A report in *The Scotsman* on 22 January 1919 informed its readers that: 'William Watters (28), West Sea Side, Prestonpans, while working at a bar coal-cutting machine in Prestongrange Colliery, was caught by the revolving bar, and received fatal injuries.'

William had been employed as a contractor at the pit. Contractors received a contract from the mine owners to produce coal in a given area. They then hired a team of men for the job and, with no discussions or negotiations, had the power to decide on their pay. These contractors were normally guilty of paying their men as little as possible, and those they hired were not allowed to discuss their wages.

There were several mines in Prestonpans at that time. Prestonlinks being the one where Geordie spent most of his working life. An article from the *Daily Worker*, 10 April 1930, indicates how bad conditions were:

NOT FIT TO WORK A WHOLE WEEK AT THE COLLIERY
Men So Speeded-Up At Prestonlinks Pit, PRESTONPANS,—No. 2 Unit, 14 West, Mine Section of Prestonlinks Pit, East Lothian, is a double unit conveyor run. The men are so speeded up that they are losing a shift every now and then, as they are not fit to go all the week. This section is supposed to be contracted by two men, who are

famous all over Scotland as the greatest slave-drivers and bullies the company ever had in their service.

I don't know how well William paid his men, but after he was killed the contract went to his brother Dave, who decided the contract would operate his way and that the workload and payments would be shared equally between him and his men. However, one of his men was heard boasting about his earnings and that led to dissatisfaction amongst those employed by other contractors who were paying their men a much lower rate. This

A family of miners in Prestonpans. Back row L–R: Geordie Watters' brothers, Dave and Tam, their cousin Arthur and his younger brother. Front Row L: Geordie's brother William. R: unknown. Photo c. 1910.

led to the other contractors asking the mine owners to take the contract from Dave. He lost the contract but, fortunately, still had a job. That was especially important as Dave and his brother Tam, both single at the time, were giving financial aid to William's widow towards the upbringing of her four young children.

Geordie was only 14 at the time this happened but memories of these events would have stayed with him for the rest of his life. He would have known at an early age that his future occupation would most definitely be in the coal mining industry, as it was for many of the lads in the town. It is little wonder that he was already looking towards socialism. In the early 1920s he joined the Territorial Army to get some military experience in the hope that he would gain some knowledge which might be useful in any future conflict, political or social.

Geordie had a deep hatred of racism and, at a time when racist views were common, he had huge respect for black American Paul Robeson. Robeson was a brilliant scholar, sportsman, a famous actor and, a singer with a voice so good that people still rave about it now, but above all, he was an outspoken fighter for the betterment of his fellow man. At the height of his fame, Robeson could sell out concert halls anywhere in the world but he would often choose to perform free at miners' galas or political rallies. He was a man of real principle and this resonated with Geordie.

On a trip to Spain to show support for the Republican government and the volunteers, Robeson visited the American Abraham Lincoln Battalion. He must have been happy to have seen that the Battalion was not segregated in the way troops were in the American army. The majority of the Battalion were white and, at a time when it was almost unthinkable for a black man to give orders to white men, they had selected black American Oliver Law as their commander.

It would have been understandable if Robeson had limited his fight to opposing the absolutely appalling treatment his own people were suffering at home in America but he realised the necessity to fight against all injustices, regardless of who it was happening to or where it was happening. He was a great role model.

Geordie always believed that employers would not improve workers' pay or working conditions voluntarily and that employees had to take strike action when necessary. He was a resolute supporter of the industrial action taken by the miners in 1921 and 1926. His outspoken support for these and other industrial actions would lead to him being blacklisted from the mining industry for many years, resulting in great hardship for him and his wife Ellen, whom he married in 1929.

In the 1930s, when the miners were still suffering greatly, due to wage cuts and increased hours, they were again considering strike action. In response to that threat the Conservative MP Lady Astor said, 'What do these earthworms want now?' That shows how little interest the Tories had in the welfare of the working class, and it is no great surprise that people like Geordie held them in such low esteem.

By the mid-1930s, Geordie was aware that the Asturian miners were in dispute with the mine owners, who were being backed by the right-wing government. In 1934, the disputes had escalated into strikes and violent clashes and there was great loss of life when the miners were brutally crushed by the Spanish Foreign Legion and the Moroccan Regulares.

Aware of the Dangers of Fascism

Geordie was an active member of the Communist Party. He would regularly speak on street corners warning about the threat fascism presented to world peace. Those who warned of these dangers were later referred to by the establishment, both in Britain and America, as 'premature anti-fascists'. He was one of many thousands who took part in the Hunger Marches.

In May 1936, despite 15,000 residents signing a petition against it, the British Union of Fascists were permitted to hold a rally in Edinburgh's Usher Hall. Outside, several thousand anti-fascist protesters were being kept apart from the fascists by a police cordon. A few of the anti-fascists, including Geordie and his friend Donald Renton from Portobello, had managed to get tickets for the event from some Edinburgh University students who were sympathetic to their cause. There were 2,500 black-shirted fascists in the hall.

The main speaker was the fascist leader and former Labour MP, Sir Oswald Mosley. As soon as he got up to speak, Geordie stood up and started to interrupt. When Mosley complained that he was being denied freedom of speech, Geordie enquired if there was freedom of speech in fascist countries. Another leading fascist on the platform was William Joyce who, during the Second World War, moved to Germany and became a propagandist for the Nazis. He became known as Lord Haw-Haw. Joyce warned Geordie that he would be forcibly ejected if he didn't shut up. Of course, Geordie didn't keep quiet and was savagely beaten up by fascist stewards before being handed over to the police, accused of being an agitator. While this was happening, Donald Renton got to his feet and sang the workers anthem, 'The Internationale'.

Geordie had been greatly outnumbered and it was reported in the press that onlookers were in a state of shock at the severity of the injuries suffered by the protesters, who had been given a real beating by the Blackshirt thugs before being thrown out of the Usher Hall. Geordie was taken to the police station in the High Street where a fascist, who had a large cut above his eye, said that Geordie was responsible for his injury. To which Geordie replied, 'I wish tae Christ it had been me, then I would have got some satisfaction.' Geordie was charged with disrupting the meeting.

In June 1936, *The Scotsman* reported that during the court case, William McNeil from Prestonpans, a witness for the accused, George Watters, said that the only reason Geordie had been ejected was that he had stood to a point of order: he had merely asked Oswald Mosley, who had been complaining about being denied freedom of speech, if the people living under fascism in Germany and Italy had freedom of speech. Jock Gilmour, who later fought alongside Geordie in the Spanish Civil War, also attended the meeting in the Usher Hall and was a witness for Geordie's defence. It came as no surprise when Geordie was found guilty. He received a £2 fine with the option of 14 days' imprisonment.

Geordie hated fascists for their racist views and their suppression of workers' rights everywhere they came to power. An article in the *Daily Worker* on Monday 18 May 1936 described the scene:

The People Against the Fascists

'Sweep Them Out! A THOUSAND people sprang to their feet shouting … Men shouted defiance from all parts of the hall… Anti-Fascist leaflets fluttered down in clouds… Three men, bleeding about the head, came out of the hall. The police outside were holding back the crowd.'

That was the picture of Mosley's meeting in Edinburgh impressed on the special correspondent not of a working-class, anti-Fascist newspaper, but of the *Scottish Daily Express*. Reports from workers who saw that beastly scene show that the brutality of the Blackshirts, the extent of the protection given to them by the police, and the furious hostility of the working people of Edinburgh were in no way different from similar sights and events at Fascist meetings in other parts of the country, from one end of these islands to the other, despite the firm and clear protest of trade unionists, who know that Fascism is the destroyer of trade unions, of Co-operators, who have seen the Co-ops of Germany and Italy smashed by Brown and Blackshirt Fascist thugs, of peace lovers who have seen Fascism pouring its poison-gas over the villages of Abyssinia – the police have been thrown into action in order to enable the Fascist baronet to thrust his unwelcome presence into the midst of decent people. After the sickening story of how Fascism sneaked into Usher Hall, Edinburgh, behind the police batons, and the fine story of how the people of Edinburgh rallied to defeat Fascism, working men and women all over the country will feel confirmed in their resolve to get together to sweep this filthy thing out of Britain.

In 2015, author and historian Daniel Gray made a series of documentaries for Scottish Television. In *People's Historian: Edinburgh Riots, part 2,* he talks about Geordie being arrested during the Usher Hall riot in 1936, and mentions that shortly after that event, Geordie had gone to Spain to fight fascism. It is interesting to note that in January 1946 William Joyce became the last person in Britain to be hanged for treason. It is almost unbelievable to learn that he claimed the Jews were responsible for the war.

In 1967 Mosley was still a well-known political figure and, during a televised interview with David Frost, he claimed that the British Union of Fascists were never anti-Jewish. The British Union of Fascists had two newspapers, *Action* and *The Blackshirt*. The archives of both are available online and a quick look at them proves that Mosley was lying.

In the 1930s, apart from the *Daily Worker*, the anti-fascists had little support from the press and the *Daily Mail* even ran the now notorious headline, 'Hurrah for the Blackshirts'. Many people are of the opinion that the *Daily Mail* is no less right wing today.

Fighting for the Spanish People

The Anglo-French Non-Intervention Policy was meant to stop other countries interfering in Spain.

Under international law, the Republican Government had a legal entitlement to buy arms but the policy prevented them from doing so, leaving them unable to fully defend themselves. The German and Italian navies were allowed to police the policy, so, flouting the pact, were able to continue stealthily supplying arms, aircraft and soldiers to Franco. Professor Paul Preston, prominent historian of the Spanish Civil War, believes this was a major factor in the eventual defeat of the Spanish Republic. When it was pointed out that the fascist rebels were being helped by Portugal, Italy and Germany, the British government said there was no evidence of this. It mystifies me how my father, a coal miner from Prestonpans, along with thousands of other working-class people, could see it to be true, but somehow the government didn't know. Geordie had a saying, 'There are none so blind as those who will not see', which I think would have been very appropriate at that time. It is worth remembering that Franco and the rest of the Spanish rebels were using arms bought with Spanish taxpayers' money to overthrow the democratically elected government.

It became evident that there was an imminent danger that Spain would be lost to the fascists. Not only would this be a disaster for the Spanish people, it would embolden the fascists on the world stage. The men who went to Spain all said that if fascism was not defeated in Spain, we would soon have to fight it here. How right they were.

Progressive people from all over the world made their way to Spain in 1936, willing to sacrifice their lives defending a government which had been improving the quality of life for the working class. Among the first to go were large numbers of German anti-fascists. If the fascists won in Spain, these men would be unable to return to their homeland as Hitler was already putting anyone who opposed him into concentration camps. These volunteers were real heroes.

Geordie decided he could not stand by and let the fascists overthrow the Progressive Front Government in Spain. He and Ellen now had three young children, George, Ellen and Billy, but Ellen fully supported his decision to go to fight fascism. It is only in recent years that I have appreciated how much my mother's support would have meant to my father. Her life would already have been extremely difficult with little money going into the house because of Geordie's long spells of unemployment due to him being blacklisted. She understood the dangers involved in his going to Spain and that he might be seriously wounded or might not come home again. However, she realised he had to stand by his beliefs and she did her bit by collecting aid for the Spanish people and in this respect she was as committed as Geordie in her support for Spain.

There was enormous interest in the events unfolding in Spain. On 13 December 1936, Independent Labour Party MP John McGovern addressed a meeting in Glasgow's City Hall. Not only was the hall filled to capacity but hundreds were unable to get in. McGovern was reporting on the findings of his visit to Spain where he had been investigating claims, by the Catholic Church and various newspapers, of alleged atrocities committed by the Republican Government. McGovern, himself a Catholic, argued that Spain was a Catholic country and the majority of the Catholics there supported the Republican government. They would not have done so if these allegations were true.

It is true to say some atrocities had been carried out by supporters of the Republican Government but none were committed before the fascists tried to overthrow the Republic. The Nationalists had been bombing civilian targets and slaughtering anyone who had supported the Republic in fascist controlled regions. All of this was supported by the all-powerful Catholic Church who were major landowners.

It would be wrong to condone the committing of atrocities by either side, yet it can be understood why Republican supporters would rise up against the supporters of fascists who were enslaving and murdering their families and friends. The Republican government was desperately trying to prevent these events from happening and at the same time fighting for its own survival against the advancing fascists. It is worth noting that while the fascists were dropping bombs on civilian areas in Madrid, none were dropped in the Salamanca district of the city where the rich lived. It was very much class warfare on the part of the fascists.

Geordie held a public meeting at Ayres Wynd in Prestonpans, asking others to join him in travelling to Spain to fight against the fascist rebels. Jimmy Kempton and Jock Gilmour bravely volunteered and the three friends travelled to Edinburgh in late December 1936, where they were joined by Donald Renton and others making their way to catch the bus to Glasgow, where they would join with comrades from all over Scotland. Many would never return.

Spain

A total of three buses full of volunteers left Glasgow that day heading to London. It is remarkable to think that most of them had never travelled abroad or had any military experience but were prepared to risk losing their lives fighting an enemy who not only had the support of the Moors, Franco's Army of Africa, considered to be the crack troops of the Nationalist Army, but also of German and Italian military units consisting of professional soldiers infinitely better armed than the Republican Army.

On their arrival in London the next obstacle was getting this large group of men, very few of them owning passports, from London to Spain. At that time you could buy a weekend pass that allowed you to visit Paris with no passport required. Needless to say, the volunteers had no intention of using their return ticket.

They spent one night in Paris before travelling to Perpignan, near the border, where they boarded a bus heading for Figueras in Spain. Just before their journey started, a border guard got on and asked to see their passports. At the front was the only volunteer with a passport and he held it up. The guard nodded and waved them on. He obviously knew what was going on and possibly even admired the men for what they were doing.

They were fortunate that they could travel to Spain this way, as those who went later had to be smuggled over the border and make a hazardous journey over the Pyrenees. They travelled from Figueras to a military barracks in Albacete, where they received a uniform plus some basic training with obsolete weapons which would have endangered their lives if they had used them.

Albacete had been under the control of the fascists before being retaken by the Republican army and some Franco supporters still remained there. In Ian MacDougall's book *Voices from the Spanish Civil War*, Geordie mentions being fired at by fascists while they were training. They had been warned that might happen and were told to report it to their Spanish comrades. The incident was reported and the Spaniards duly dealt with the situation.

Geordie described their food rations as being adequate, if not plentiful and said that none of them complained, as they had agreed that feeding the

Spanish children should be the priority. This attitude is another indication of the character of the men who went to Spain.

After a stay of about a week in Albacete they were sent to Madrigueras for more advanced training, and here they met Jock Cunningham and Tom Wintringham for the first time. These men were two of the leading members of the soon-to-be formed xv Brigade. Geordie was very impressed by both these men. He later spoke about Cunningham catching a member of the Brigade striking and bullying a young volunteer. Cunningham gathered the men and said that it was time to do some teaching. He challenged the loudmouth bully about his behaviour. When he showed no remorse and continued his bullying behaviour, Cunningham proceeded to give him a real beating. He made it clear to the men that they were there for one reason only: to fight fascism. Bullying would not be tolerated.

When the International Brigades arrived in Spain they received a great reception from the Spanish people. Thousands of volunteers had travelled from all over the world to fight for Spain's democracy, and that was greatly appreciated by the Spaniards.

One of the things that left Geordie elated was hearing the different nationalities singing the workers anthem, 'The Internationale', in their own languages. Decades later, when he rarely spoke of his participation in the war, he would still talk about the thrill of hearing that wonderful sound. Another Scottish volunteer, John Dunlop, later described hearing the same thing as the greatest moment of his life. My favourite quote by Dunlop was regarding the number of volunteers who were from working class backgrounds. He said that in all his time in Spain he'd only seen one middle class volunteer, and that was himself.

Later during training, they were instructed on how to use Lewis machine guns and Russian Maxim machine guns and were issued with Russian rifles. Donald Renton was particularly pleased with this, not just because they were hugely superior to the ones they had been issued previously; he also liked the fact that they had a hammer and sickle engraved on them.

Around this time there was tension among some of the Irish volunteers, many of whom had been involved in the fight against British rule in their own country. A problem arose when George Nathan, one of the commanders, was recognised as someone who had served in Ireland as part of the British army. Nathan defused the situation to a certain extent by insisting they were all there for the same reason, to fight fascism. However, some Irish volunteers later chose to fight with the Abraham Lincoln Battalion rather than the British Battalion.

Geordie was to be a part of the Saklatvala Battalion's No. 2 Machine Gun Company, along with Jock Gilmour, Tommy Bloomfield, Donald Renton, Archie Williams, Jimmy Rutherford, Jimmy Maley, Bert Levy, Ted Dickenson and others, under the command of Harold Fry. Fry insisted on a strict no-alcohol rule. He even checked the water bottles to make sure there was no contraband. The wisdom of such a policy became obvious a short time later when the Company suffered a disastrous incident caused by one man's drunkenness.

Geordie was Political Delegate and Section Secretary for No. 2 Machine Gun Company's Section 6, and was on the committee. In a report in the Moscow Archives, he was described as 'a good influence'. Donald Renton was Political Commissar for their Company. By the 12 February 1937, their very basic training had been completed and they were advanced to the front line at Jarama, where the fascists were rapidly advancing towards Madrid. It was vital the men kept the Madrid road open to ensure supplies to the capital.

The International Brigade was made up of a large group of volunteers, most of whom had never handled a gun before leaving home. They were being thrown into fierce battles against a highly trained enemy which consisted of Moors, German and Italian military units, with air support. In other words, the enemy were more numerous, better-armed and battle-hardened.

Jarama, Day 1

On 12 February 1937, alongside Harold Fry's heavy Machine Gun Company, Tom Wintringham had sent three other companies into action. They were No. 1 Company, commanded by Kit Conway, No. 3 Company commanded by William Briskey and No. 4 Company, under the command of Bert Overton. Ahead of them were the Franco-Belges, who were being fiercely bombarded by the advancing fascists but were still holding the line, resulting in great loss to themselves.

The previous day the ammunition for the machine guns had been in cases which were handed over to the battalion by the brigade quartermaster. No one noticed that the cases contained the correct type of belts but the wrong type of cartridges. (Incidentally, there were suggestions of sabotage but these claims were never validated.) The ammunition was loaded onto a lorry and Captain Wintringham put Sergeant Hornsby in charge of it, telling him to stay with the truck to protect it. On the morning of 12 February, Hornsby, apparently afraid of what was ahead of him, had several alcoholic drinks before he set off. He then drove the lorry out towards the front where the machine guns were to be positioned.

However, under the effect of the alcohol, Hornsby overturned the lorry several miles from the front and a man was killed during the accident. (Hornsby was later put on trial for this.) It was said that he was responsible for the further loss of 180 men that day, as the Battalion had no support from their Machine Gun Company who, because of the delay and the wait for the correct ammunition to be loaded into the belts, were out of action for five hours. During that time the machine-gunners only had the use of their rifles.

Fry's Machine Gun Company had endured a real struggle getting their heavy guns up the very steep slope to get to their chosen position. All this while being bombarded by enemy fire, resulting in heavy loss of men. One of the first of these casualties was Jock Gilmour, Geordie's friend from Prestonpans. Jock was very badly wounded and had been advised to wait for an ambulance but he insisted the ambulances should be used by others whom he considered to be more seriously wounded than himself. His concern for his comrades cost him his life: he died as a result of loss of blood. He had willingly given his life fighting for the Spanish people and should be remembered for his courage. I don't know if, in the midst of the battle, Geordie knew that his friend was dead or, if he later regretted encouraging and recruiting Jock. Without doubt that was something he would have asked of himself in the years to come but, of course, he knew that Jock had gone knowingly and willingly to fight for the cause.

When the Company got their guns into position, and after resting for a few minutes, they discovered to their horror that they had been supplied with ammunition for modern German Maxims instead of the WW1 German Maxims which they had been given. It is fair to say the first day in action was not going well.

When the correct ammunition eventually arrived it had to be filled into the belts, but the wrong ammunition had to be removed from them first, a laborious and time-consuming task. They also needed picks and shovels to dig in their guns but the supply of those items was totally inadequate, which meant that they were unable to protect themselves properly. During that period, the No. 2 Machine Gun Company was being protected from the front by Overton's No. 4 Company and from the rear by Conway's No. 1 Company.

Things improved considerably for Fry's Company some hours later, after the correct cartridges arrived and the belts were filled. At that point, Wintringham gave permission for Overton's No. 4 Company to retreat because of the heavy losses they were suffering. In his book *English Captain*, Wintringham described the events that followed:

> Then the Moors boiled over Suicide Hill, over the crest in a dense line, spread on to the slopes where Overton's reserve section had been, and headed down into the grass valley. And Fry's guns woke. As soon as the slashing crackle of Maxims came back to us I stood up and saw what every machine-gunner longs for, and seldom sees, enemy infantry bunched in the open, with a skyline behind them and no good cover available. Fry made the most of this target. He let the Moors come over the hill; his taut gunners could hear them yelling. A few Moors were firing rifles and machine-rifles from the hip as they ran, but firing wildly without knowing where the English were. Fry let them come down the slope, find their retreating opponents, and begin to turn their fire south toward the fringe of olive trees. Some lay down; others in their excitement stood still and fired from the shoulder; others were flowing down to the valley. Fry's fire hit them from an unexpected angle; within 60 seconds his five guns had put over a thousand bullets amongst the Moors. Four of his guns reached the end of their belts together; the fifth came to silence as the first of the four started tearing away at a new belt. Fry himself was using a rifle as were his ammunition carriers. The Spanish colts had started in, with the deep decided note their heavy barrels give them; when they stopped, all too soon, I could hear the two guns detached from Fry's company beyond the colts. A flood of fire was covering the retirement of the three companies. The Moors could not reply; few could get their machine-rifles to the range before one of Fry's gunners got them. The German heavy machine gunners had not reached the hill; their fire had died off because they were shifting their guns up. Only the Moors on the knoll to our right front knew Fry's position with the accuracy that follows hours of watching; but their fire was ineffective; not an English gunner ducked for it. After three or four

minutes about half the Moors who had flooded over Suicide Hill had tried to run back over it; caught by two of Fry's guns traversing along the skyline they had gone down in little heaps of dead and wounded. The remainder of the Moors dropped into tiny patches of cover from which they could not stir without attracting bullets. Scarcely any were using their rifles. And the survivors of our three companies were coming level with us to our left. They had passed the deepest point of the valley and were climbing towards the sunken road.

In the evening the men received a visit from Wintringham, who later wrote that he was well satisfied with the 'we'll show them attitude' of Fry's men. That night, when Wintringham was surveying the front, he heard a distant voice calling for help and, though he thought it could be one of their own wounded, it was possibly a trap by the enemy, who would know they were fighting an English-speaking battalion. Reluctantly, he decided it was too risky to send out a rescue party and instructed Fry not to risk his men by attempting a rescue. In his original notes, which can be found in the Moscow Archives, Wintringham wrote:

war is the most hateful thing I know and there listening alone in the dark when I made the decision to let our wounded lie I knew a good measure of its beastliness.

However, a small group of volunteers insisted they had to attempt to rescue their wounded comrade. Fry, going against Wintringham's strict orders, allowed them to go out to search for the man. Bill Meredith later commented in the Brigade Bulletin that he had seen one of the bravest deeds ever that night, when these three heroes went out in the pitch blackness to rescue their comrade and, due to the close proximity of the enemy, facing almost certain death. Unfortunately, their mission was fruitless. Earlier in the day, several men had been rescued under heavy fire and Geordie Watters had been involved in both rescue missions. These brave actions are described in a letter from Donald Renton published on 30 August 1937, in the *Daily Worker*, sent in response to an account of events written by Fred Copeman.

Praise for a Spain Hero

Copeman's account of the battle of Jarama brings back to mind many of the incidents he has described.

That heart-breaking moment of arrival at the scene of action to find that no ammunition had been brought forward, and that our maxims were therefore so much useless lumber, will live forever in the memories of those who experienced it.

What Fred has failed to do in recounting the heroism of others is to describe how, although badly wounded, he succeeded in bringing up the material we required to demonstrate the skill we had gained in the use of the guns as a result of his instruction.

Indeed, this aspect of his work has never been commented upon at any time. Supplied with the maxims the night before we left the base for our front, our time on the train and a few hours at Villarubia were spent in mastering the stoppages and in obtaining a general knowledge of the guns. That we were able to achieve this object speaks volumes for his technical abilities as a military instructor.

He may recollect, as a matter of fact, how we were able to snatch a little time for a Company concert, at which he rendered 'Popeye, the Sailor Man' with great gusto. The hero of Invergordon, and many a blood-scarred battlefield in Spain, can be very human indeed. It may be of general interest to your readers to know that the comrade mainly responsible for the effort to rescue the wounded comrade whose cries we heard was George Watters, of Prestonpans, who earlier in the day, with Tommy Degnan, Political Commissar of No. 3 Company, had brought in a number of wounded under fire.

Tommy is now in a base hospital wounded through the lungs, while Geordie's health has suffered severely, as a result of the ordeal he underwent while a prisoner in Franco's jails. The history of the British Battalion would not be complete without their names.

What Donald did not mention was that he himself was one of the men Geordie rescued that day.

In *Voices From the Spanish Civil War*, Donald Renton makes an excellent point about the Allied Agreement at Potsdam to destroy fascism everywhere, asking why 'everywhere' didn't include Spain.

Some months after the Battle of Jarama, Bert 'Yank' Levy sent a letter to Wintringham informing him of an incident that had happened about noon on 12 February 1937. Bert Overton, Commander of No. 4 Company, had run to the ledge where Fry's Company were positioned. Overton was minus his puttees and shoes, presumably to help him run without slipping on the muddy ground. Fry enquired what he was doing there and Overton replied that he was looking for instructions. Fry then asked where his Company was, to which Overton replied, 'I don't know, I don't know'. Fry then instructed him to get back to his men, which he did after resting for about 20 minutes. Overton was not coping well with the terrible situation and, considering the position they were holding was referred to by the entire battalion as Suicide Hill, it is easy to understand why.

Jarama, Day 2

On 13 February, Wintringham set off early in the morning to prepare his troops in readiness for another fascist attack. To guard Fry's right flank, Overton's No. 4 Co. was posted exactly on a line with No. 2 Co. and 100 yards to the right.

A day of drama began with the sound of No. 2 Company's guns, so loud that Wintringham thought a fascist attack was in progress. Then a runner informed Wintringham that the valley was flooded with Moors and men in khaki, falangists, and that Comrade Fry thought there was the best part of a brigade. They were well down the valley and running like hell. 'Towards us?' enquired Wintringham. 'Gawd no, they are running for cover!' was the reply. Fry's guns were slaughtering them for a full 20 minutes till all their gun belts were empty.

A new brigade of fascists consisting of both Moors and falangists had arrived during the night and had decided to sleep in the valley, thinking it was safe because there had been no action in that area so far that night. That proved to be a fatal error for most of them; safe to say it was a great start to the day for the antifascists.

However, in spite of No. 2 Company killing very large numbers of the enemy, it remained the case that the enemy were much more numerous and infinitely better armed. Wintringham reckoned that the fascists had 40 brand new Maxim machine guns compared to the six 20-odd-year-old WW1 Maxims that Fry's men possessed. In his book *English Captain* Wintringham describes No. 2 Machine Gun Company as 'these hand-picked men'.

That afternoon, disaster was to befall No. 2 Company. What happened was detailed in Levy's letter to Wintringham. At about 3pm, the enemy dropped two shells on the plateau to their right. Looking in that direction, Levy was amazed to see No. 4 Company running at full pelt to their rear with their commander, Overton, leading them by about 25 yards.

About 90 minutes later, Overton sent a message to Fry requesting that Fry's Company retire to the rear. Fry ignored the request, as he was aware that Overton had lost his nerve on two previous occasions and No. 2 Company had already been given very strict orders to hold their position at all costs. This was followed by a visit from Wintringham, who again confirmed the order to hold. After Wintringham had left the area, Overton sent another message asking that Fry retire No. 2 Company. Fry rejected this request again. Shortly after this, Levy looked over to their right flank where No. 4 Company should have been and saw that it had been occupied by a large number of fascists. Wintringham later said that if Fry had reported how Overton had behaved on the 12th, he would not have trusted him to guard Fry's right flank the following day. Wintringham had twice been assured by Overton that he had left men guarding Fry's right flank; this was a lie and it was to lead to Fry's No. 2 Company being surrounded and captured.

No. 2 Company were being attacked from the front and Levy saw several of his comrades fall down dead for no obvious reason. They had not realised that the fascists had managed to come up behind them and that he and his comrades were also being attacked from the rear. Geordie was firing one of the guns to the front when a fascist hit him on the back of his head with the butt of his rifle, knocking him out. When he regained consciousness, his comrades had their hands in the air and were surrounded by fascists. They were now prisoners of Franco.

How ferocious the fighting had been on those days in Jarama Valley is shown by the fact that after only two days, No. 2 Machine Gun Company had lost well over 50 per cent of their men, killed, wounded or missing, and their battalion had gone from 600 men to approximately 200. In comparison, percentage-wise, the British army lost 12.5 per cent of their men during the six years of the Second World War.

Overton was sentenced to ten years in prison for his actions but his sentence was later commuted and he was given a job supplying ammunition to the front. He lost his life shortly afterwards while doing that job. It would be easy to criticise his behaviour at Jarama but he simply lost his nerve. Nowadays that would be classed as suffering from shell-shock. Being aware of Overton's problems, Fry should have reported him to Wintringham as this would have resulted in a better outcome for Overton and so many others.

At the time of No. 2 Company's capture, Bill Meredith, a company scout, not realising what was happening to his comrades, was returning to Fry's Company when Levy, who had just been captured, noticed him and shouted a warning to him to run away. In an article in the *Daily Worker*, Meredith stated that Levy's warning had saved his life that day but, only a few months later Meredith became another victim of the war when he was killed at the battle of Brunete.

Earlier the previous day, No. 1 Company also had a devastating incident when their commander, the legendary Irish fighter Kit Conway, lost his life along with a large number of his men.

In an interview published in the *Liverpool Echo* on 1 June 1937, James Pugh stated that, on 13 February, after No. 2 Machine Gun Company were surrounded and there were only 40 of them left, the men surrendered; but even then, the fascists continued shooting and knifing them to death and only 27 survived and were taken prisoner.

Franco's Prisoners

The men were being taken to a temporary holding-place for prisoners at San Martin de la Vega. After a few minutes' marching, they were handed over to a division of the Moors' Cavalry. At one stage they had been lined up, expecting to be shot, when they were asked if they were Russian. One of their captors realised that they were British and they were spared execution. During their capture, Harold Fry had been wounded in the right arm and many others had been badly wounded. It did not take them long to discover that their lives were still in great danger.

Each man was tied to one other prisoner, their thumbs bound together with a piece of field telephone wire. Geordie was tied to Tommy Bloomfield. The prisoners were tied to horses and forcibly marched for about 5 kilometres, pushed along by the vicious Moorish cavalry, who were using their rifle butts and whips, and even biting into the prisoners' necks with their teeth.

Philip Ellis had asked one of their captors if he could have a cigarette. He had been told yes, but, when he put his hand into his pocket to take out the cigarette, the same guard raised his sub-machine gun and shot him. Not only was Ellis killed, but another comrade lost his life at the same time. John Stevens, standing immediately behind Ellis, had been hit by a bullet from the same gun.

Fry's second in command, Ted Dickenson, had torn Fry's officer's braids from his arm but did not have time to remove his own stripes, which immediately identified him as an officer. The prisoners were asked why Fry had a different uniform from the others and they were asked if he was an officer too. The men claimed he was a clerk, which meant he had a different uniform from them, and that saved his life at the time. After walking for about ten minutes, Dickenson was separated from the others and told to stand in front of a tree. Dickenson marched up to the tree, turned around, stood upright and, while saluting his comrades with a clenched fist, was executed. In a very short period of time he had saved Fry's life and then his own life had ended in the most heroic way imaginable. Geordie rarely mentioned his time in Spain but I can remember several occasions when he mentioned the dignified manner in which Dickenson had faced his death.

When they arrived at San Martin de la Vega, the men were put into a small room along with two French prisoners, who were taken out and executed shortly afterwards. They received no food or medical treatment during their time there. A priest visited them during the night and said they would all be shot in the morning. Although that did not happen, the fascists' total disregard for the prisoners' lives must have terrified the men.

Next day the prisoners were loaded onto trucks (known as camions) to be transported to Navalcarnero. In *Voices from the Spanish Civil War*, Geordie described what he thought of as 'an amusing incident'. When they were passing through a big town, a fascist supporter started shouting at them and threatening them with a large club. Geordie turned to Tommy Bloomfield and said, 'He looks like a right cheery bastard.' It is good to know that, in spite of being in such a dire situation, they still managed to express their contempt for the fascists.

They were held in Navalcarnero for four days, nine men in each cell. The cells were filthy and even contained human dirt. The men did receive one meal a day, consisting of beans in oil plus a piece of stale bread. According to Jimmy Rutherford's report on their treatment, they received five or six beatings a day from the Moors during their time there. Each man was thoroughly interrogated by a Spanish officer who could speak English and he actually treated them civilly. After four days, they were taken to a concentration camp in Talavera de la Reina. In Richard Baxell's book *Unlikely Warriors*, he writes that, at this stage, they had still received no medical treatment for their men who had been wounded at Jarama: Harold Fry had a broken arm, Donald Renton had leg wounds and Jimmy Rutherford and Geordie Watters had been beaten virtually unconscious.

Their prison was a further 80 kilometres inside fascist controlled territory and they would spend almost three months of their lives there. The wounded were taken to a hospital and received some treatment for their wounds, but the hospital was as dirty as the prison. The prison was an old pottery factory that housed 200 prisoners. They had no mattresses or blankets and the guards had taken away any warm clothing they had owned. The prisoners were freezing, covered in lice, and mice ran over them while they slept.

Tommy Bloomfield said they were constantly subjected to mental torture. The guards would tell them, 'Esta tarde todos muerto' – 'This afternoon you all die.' Then in the evening, 'Esta noche todos muerto' – 'Tonight you all die.' This is not something I ever heard Geordie speak about, but it would be something he would never forget.

At night after the men who were to be executed were taken away by guards, those who remained were told 'Mañana por a la mañana' – by which they meant 'Tomorrow morning you all die.' It was obvious that the fascists were not guilty of making idle threats as many other prisoners were murdered. The men must have been absolutely terrified.

AC Williams, a member of No. 2 Company, kept a diary while he was there. Thanks to him, we know that Geordie landed in the hospital with stomach, eye and dental problems, all due to the extremely brutal treatment, malnourishment and filthy conditions in the prisons. In the photos of him in Spain he isn't wearing glasses, but after he was released from Franco's jail he needed thick lenses for the remainder of his life, a visible legacy of the ill-treatment.

After about six weeks, they were visited by a group of civilians, one of them said he was an English Consul. On hearing this, the men asked if he could be of assistance to them. His reply was that he was not there in any official capacity so could not help, and also, that their plight was of no interest to him personally.

Jimmy Rutherford said they received a visit from the British Consul, a man who claimed to be very sympathetic to their plight. He interviewed them and, as he left, told them he would do something to help. Jimmy recalled that he did supply one shaving kit with no spare blades, to be shared by all the British prisoners. That was not really much of a help. Reports from the men differ in ways, but all agree there was no real help from the Consul.

Another day they were all interviewed by Don Pablo Merry del Val, an English-speaking Spaniard. After interviews lasting one hour per prisoner, they were told that there was only one way to avoid being executed and that was to fight for the fascists. In spite of the fact that the prisoners would realise it was almost inevitable that they would all be taken out and executed, none of them accepted this offer. Prisoners being shot there was a regular occurrence but the men would never fight for Franco.

By this time, their families were aware that their loved ones were missing in action and, with good reason, would be fearing the worst. Geordie's wife Ellen feared he was dead but just had to carry on with life as usual for the sake of the children. She was in no financial position to buy luxuries such as a fancy framed photo but, probably thanks to Dependants' Aid, Ellen went to a photographic studio and had a portrait taken along with her three children, George, Ellen and Billy. The photographer then added Geordie's image, no mean feat with no photo-editing software available; the pencil marks are still visible on the photo where Geordie's image was added! Ellen now had a beautiful photograph of herself, her husband and their children to remember him by.

In the meantime, even though they thought Geordie was probably dead, Ellen's brother Willie Dickson was making arrangements to go to fight for the Spanish Republican Government.

Some of the prisoners, with the help of Spanish comrades, tried to improve their grasp of Spanish, but it became rather pointless due to the short time between Spanish prisoners arriving and then being taken away and executed.

One of the horrible jobs the No. 2 Company men were forced to do was digging mass graves for prisoners the fascists had executed. There were about 30 executions a day, but the number of prisoners remained at 200 as new prisoners were arriving daily; both men and women were victims of these atrocities, no one was safe. They never knew who was going to be taken away next.

A short time after they arrived at Talavera de la Reina, reporters from the British press visited the prison and took photographs of them. The journalists wanted interviews too but, probably because the men believed that the British newspapers, with their links to the fascists, were not to be trusted, they refused to co-operate.

On 23 March 1937, a film crew turned up to record footage of the prisoners for a newsreel which was shown in British cinemas on 29 March. The footage shows Geordie talking to the guard and can be found on YouTube.

Giving the misleading impression that they were treating the men well, the guards gave the prisoners cigarettes and food. However not all the men had been given matches and after filming finished, the guards took back the cigarettes. The English narrator of the film falsely said of the men:

> Some of the army of unemployed, enrolled for road making under the Spanish Government but captured by the insurgents and now being filmed in this detention camp being served with food, of which there is no scarcity.

The filmmakers did not show the lice that covered their clothes and bodies, nor did they record the filthy conditions in which they were confined. They did not show that the men were starving and ill, and still suffering from regular beatings. It was merely a propaganda film.

One day in late March 1937, Ellen had an unexpected visit from a neighbour. She said she had just been at the cinema and had seen a newsreel item showing some British men who had been taken prisoner by the fascists in Spain and, to her surprise, she had spotted Geordie Watters. Ellen was very excited by this amazing news and rushed to get on the next bus to the cinema; the projectionist was kind enough to put the newsreel back on, and it was confirmed that it was indeed Geordie! By coincidence, that was how many of the prisoners' families found out that their loved ones were still alive; albeit they were still in extreme danger.

In May, the men were transferred to a prison in Salamanca, where they were put on trial. This prison held about 3,000 prisoners; nearly all of them had been sentenced to death. Fry's men were put on trial, charged with military rebellion. Ironically, the charges were brought by fascists who were themselves engaged in a military rebellion against Spain's democratically elected government. The trial was conducted in Spanish but the accused were given an interpreter who could not speak English. In the public gallery, among the spectators, were a substantial number of priests who, according to Donald Renton in *Voices from the Spanish Civil War*, were gloating at the prospect of the harsh sentences likely to be handed down to the men. Perhaps that was an indication of how unlikely it was that they would receive a fair trial. Not surprisingly the punishment for the accused was extremely harsh. Five were sentenced to death: George Leeson, Maurice Goldberg, Harold Fry, Jimmy Rutherford and Charles West. Geordie Watters and George Stuhldreer were sentenced to life in solitary confinement and the others were sentenced to 30 years. They were then moved to the New Model Prison, also in Salamanca.

In almost three months as Franco's prisoners, they had been starved, beaten and subjected to conditions that would permanently damage their health. And, the fear and stress caused by being sentenced to death, or spending 30 years or longer in that prison hell-hole, would have put the most terrible strain on even the strongest of personalities. One day, a young prisoner who had been sentenced to death lost his nerve and was pleading with the guards for mercy. Geordie offered to take his place and the guards accepted his offer. Geordie was given three days to get his affairs in order, after which he was to be executed.

I had never heard of that incident until my daughter, Angela, read about it on the internet site Communist Biographies. I asked my older brother, Jimmy, if he knew about these events. He said he did know and that, many years ago, he had asked Dad why he had volunteered to take the lad's place. Dad replied that he had felt empathy with the lad and he was so ill himself that he thought it was very likely he was going to die there anyway. And so he thought it would be better to give the lad a chance to survive. A number of his fellow prisoners had already died due to the harsh conditions.

Meanwhile, a chain of events was happening elsewhere that would lead to their freedom. The International Brigade had made it known to the fascists that if they continued to execute IB prisoners, they would take similar action against their fascist prisoners, including Italians and Germans.

The prisoners were unaware that negotiations were taking place at the League of Nations to secure their freedom as part of a prisoner exchange involving them and Italian fascists captured by the Republicans, and it was not until negotiations were nearing completion that they were told. Considering the fact these negotiations had been going on for some time, could their trials and death sentences have been mind-games played by their vicious captors? The fascists frequently executed prisoners from other countries but had agreed to an exchange of British prisoners. The fascists were benefiting from the Anglo-French Non-Intervention Policy by covertly supplying arms to Franco. So, could it be the case that perhaps the fascists didn't want to risk upsetting the British, and thereby losing the advantage gained by the enforcement of the Anglo-French policy? Maybe the Non-Intervention Policy had inadvertently saved the mens' lives.

The men were warned that, should they be released in a prisoner exchange, they must not return to Spain to continue their fight. In the event of recapture they would be executed. To make it easier to identify them in future, they had their fingerprints taken. This was later to prove disastrous for young Jimmy Rutherford.

The world was spiralling towards another world war but, at the beginning of 1937, the right wing media had been full of articles about the upcoming coronation of George VI and his wife Elizabeth, as king and queen of the United Kingdom and the Dominions of the British Commonwealth, and as emperor and empress of India. The coronation took place at Westminster Abbey on 12 May 1937. The media was in a frenzy and the attire of the king and queen and their guests was of more interest to them than the plight of Geordie and his comrades. Geordie certainly would have had no interest in those events, he had no liking for royalty.

Once the prisoner exchange had been agreed the fascists supplied the men with clothing so as to make it appear that they had been well treated. This provision consisted of a very thin, poor quality civilian suit. On the day of the exchange, George Leeson and Maurice Goldberg were held back. It was heartbreaking for the men to leave their comrades behind, facing an uncertain future.

The exchange prisoners were taken from Salamanca to Irun, on the Spanish border, where they were paraded through crowds of fascist supporters, all giving the fascist salute. Just as they were about to cross the border to France and freedom, the men were ordered to give the same salute in response, or they would be returned to prison. The men had no desire to give the fascist salute but neither did they want to be sent back to prison so, after some discussion, the men decided that only one of them would make the salute. The fascists agreed to this plan and George Stuhldreer was chosen as their representative. He gave the fascist salute and only then were they allowed to cross the border.

Unknown to Geordie, his wife's brother, William Dickson, from Musselburgh, had arrived in Spain just a few days earlier to fight the fascists.

On 29 May 1937, just as the released prisoners were on their way home, the German cruiser *Deutschland* was attacked in the port of Ibiza. The cruiser was said to be part of the International Non-Intervention Committee Patrol. Two Soviet bombers, part of the Republican Air Force, allegedly mistook it for a Nationalist fighter ship. Their bombs caused fires on the ship, killing 31 sailors and wounding many others. The Germans were furious and their warship, *Admiral Scheer*, took its revenge by shelling the Republican-held city of Almeria, causing enormous damage. Because of the bombing of the *Deutschland*, Germany and Italy then withdrew from the meetings of the Non-Intervention Committee. Perhaps if these events had happened even a day or two earlier, the prisoner exchange might not have gone ahead.

The Prisoners Return Home

On 29 May 1937, the released men left Paris to catch the steamship *Versailles* to Newhaven Docks, arriving there next morning. They then travelled by a continental boat train to Victoria Station where several members of the press were waiting for them. A reporter from the *Daily Herald* described what he found as '23 men, haggard and half starved, and haunted by having to leave two of their group behind in Spain with death sentences hanging over them.' (The two men were eventually released, but not till many months later.)

The group photo of Geordie and others giving an anti-fascist salute shows that my father, who was of a naturally small and wiry build and had been in very good physical condition when he went to Spain, had been reduced to skin and bone. It was obvious from the photos that all the prisoners had suffered extreme weight loss.

One of the prisoners, Yank Levy, told reporters that the treatment they had received from the fascists was terrible. When a reporter pointed out that a fascist spokesperson had stated that they had been well treated, Yank replied that he would like to meet that man and ram that lie back down his throat, as they were practically starving in Talavera. They had one bowl of water between the lot of them to wash in and had to grovel in the dirt; they were covered in filth with no means of keeping clean. The toilet facilities

'A salute from captured British members of the International Column, released from rebel Spain, on their arrival at Victoria Station yesterday', pictured in *The Daily Herald*, 31 May 1937. Geordie Watters third from right.

were horrendous with no way to wash their hands before eating so, as no cutlery was supplied, any food they received was handled with filthy hands. He added that, during the three months they were held prisoner, they slept on the ground with no straw or covers and ten of his comrades had died in that camp from lung disease contracted there.

When Geordie got home to Prestonpans, he learned that Willie Dickson had joined the International Brigade and was already in Spain. He would have known how many Internationals were losing their lives there, and that Geordie had been missing, so he showed great courage in going. Willie had left behind a wife and two young children. Sadly, Willie lost his life early in July during the battle of Brunete. Donald Renton's brother-in-law, Bill Cranston, was in the trench with Willie and an officer, Jack Black, at the time. Bill later remarked that when Jack and Prestonpans boy, Bill Dickson, were killed, that was one time he felt really afraid in Spain, and it was only a matter of luck that it had not been him. He said they were both good lads. *The Musselburgh News* reported Willie's death on 27 August 1937.

Musselburgh Man Killed in Spain

Mrs Wm. Dickson, of 136 Rothesay Place, Musselburgh, was notified at the weekend that her husband had been killed in the Spanish War.

Together with the report she received her husband's identity card, pay book and return of personal letters. Mr Dickson, who was 26, leaves, in addition to his wife, two children.

Mr Wm. Dickson was a son of Mr and Mrs Wm. Dickson, of 41 Eskview Avenue, Musselburgh, and used to work with his father who is the foreman of a squad of workmen engaged laying electric cables. He had been unemployed for some months before leaving for Spain about four months ago.

The father states his son left unknown to him to fight with the Spanish Government forces. From Spain he wrote cheering letters to his mother as well as his wife. Mr Dickson says that as a ban exists on volunteers from this country going to Spain his son must have been smuggled across, and to those responsible for this act he lays the blame in the first instance for his son's death. He would like to see them discovered and punished. His son, he said, was not a Communist.

WIDOW'S STATEMENT

Mrs Dickson, the widow, says her husband went to Spain with her full agreement. He made application to be allowed to go to Spain as early as November, but was only successful in April of this year. His reason for going, she said, was because of his intense hatred of fascism and his love of freedom and democracy, and to them who assisted him in getting to Spain she held nothing but respect for the noble work they were carrying on. She intended to take up the work her husband had been doing before he went to Spain in acting on the Spanish Aid Committee.

William Dickson

Reading that statement filled me with great admiration for my aunt who, in spite of her own loss, still intended to help the Spanish people.

Willie's father sent a letter to the local press angrily blaming Geordie's influence for Willie's decision to go to Spain. I know that Geordie sent a reply to the newspaper addressing the accusation.

Ironically Willie and Ellen's father, William John Dickson, was to spend many years of his life living with Geordie and Ellen. He was an extremely unpleasant man and I have never heard anyone say a good word about him. As children we never referred to him as grandfather, only as 'auld Dickson' and avoided him as much as possible. It shows the type of man Geordie was to have put up with him in his family home for so long. Maybe Geordie felt some sympathy towards him for losing his son in Spain in 1937. Not long after that, another son, 22-year-old James, who was in the RAF, died in Italy during the Second World War.

As Donald Renton stated in the letter sent to the *Daily Worker* three months after their return, Geordie's health was still greatly impaired. However, this may have saved his life as, if he had been fully fit, it was likely that he would have returned to Spain, as did several of his comrades. Two were good friends of his from Edinburgh, Harold Fry and Jimmy Rutherford, both of whom had been sentenced to death but were later released in the prisoner exchange. Back in Spain, Fry was made a commander and Rutherford was to be given officer training. Both lost their lives shortly after returning. Harold Fry was killed fighting on the front line. His wife later said that nothing could have stopped Harold from returning to Spain, and she would never have tried to stop him. She was obviously very supportive of him and the fight against fascism. Jimmy Rutherford was among a group of men captured by the fascists. He was interviewed by Merry del Val and, even though Jimmy's comrades had given him a different name, Merry del Val recognised him from the first time he had been captured. His fingerprints were checked and Jimmy was executed.

Tommy Bloomfield was another prisoner to return to Spain. His mother wrote a letter to Peter Kerrigan expressing her concerns for Tommy's welfare, and broke the sad news that Tommy's four-year-old brother, who Tommy was devoted to, had been scalded to death in an accident which had been caused by a drunk neighbour. She said the tragedy was due to the misuse of an unsafe boiler in the dreadful housing conditions they were living in.

She told Peter of her hatred of capitalism and how it was ruining lives. Although she had no money to spare, she included a parcel of cigarettes for the comrades in the Battalion. On 23 September 1938, Peter replied from a hospital in Barcelona where he was recovering from a slight hand wound. He told her he was very sorry to hear of her loss and, as it appeared from her letter that she did not want to tell Tommy herself, he would tell him the sad news as gently as possible when he next saw him. As for Tommy's welfare, he said they had spoken fairly recently and Tommy had told him all about her and how she was a great supporter of the Spanish cause. Peter told her that Tommy was not at the front at the moment and it looked as if the men would be returning to their homes very soon, so she should not worry.

Peter Kerrigan received many letters from people desperately begging for information about family members who had travelled to Spain. They told him about family members at home who were ill and dying and wanted to see their son or husband one more time. Often, he had to tell them the sad news that their loved one was not coming home.

Tommy, who survived the war, sang the praises of those brave men he fought alongside but never mentioned his own enormous contribution to their cause. Late in life Tommy said, 'Today – well, I don't have much money, but I am rich, very rich, in the people I have known.' What a beautiful tribute to his comrades.

In spite of huge losses, the volunteers continued to fight alongside the equally courageous Spanish army but the odds were stacked against them. It became obvious that as long as Franco had the support of German and Italian military units he would win the war. In 1938 the Republican government requested that the Internationals leave Spain, in the hope that the fascists would do the same with their German and Italian supporters.

Before they left in October 1938, the International Brigades were honoured with a farewell parade through Barcelona, where huge crowds of emotional Spaniards waved them farewell. It was here that La Pasionaria, Dolores Ibárruri, who had inspired the International Brigades' battle-cry of 'No Pasaran' (They Shall Not Pass), made her famous speech which began:

> It is very difficult to say a few words in farewell to the heroes of
> the International Brigades, because of what they are and what they
> represent. A feeling of sorrow, an infinite grief catches our throat –
> sorrow for those who are going away, for the soldiers of the highest
> ideal of human redemption, exiles from their countries, persecuted
> by the tyrants of all peoples – grief for those who will stay here

forever mingled with the Spanish soil, in the very depth of our heart, hallowed by our feeling of eternal gratitude.

And, after a very long emotional speech of thanks, she ended with the words:

We shall not forget you; and, when the olive tree of peace is in flower, entwined with the victory laurels of the Republic of Spain – return!

Return to our side for here you will find a homeland – those who have no country or friends, who must live deprived of friendship – all, all will have the affection and gratitude of the Spanish people who today and tomorrow will shout with enthusiasm. – Long live the heroes of the International Brigades!

Compare her beautiful tribute to these brave men with the following quote from Winston Churchill's son, the Tory MP Randolph Churchill:

A few excitable Catholics and ardent Socialists (in Britain) think that this war matters, but for the general public it's just a lot of bloody dagoes killing each other.

With the Churchills it was 'like father like son'.

After the war, Franco's dictatorship terrorised the Spanish people. Many who had fought for their Popular Front government were shot as traitors or put into camps and used as slave labour. For decades, the fascist government continued to commit atrocities against women from families who had supported the Republican government. In later years, when these women became pregnant and went to hospital to give birth, they were told their babies had died. However, this was not the case – the babies were being adopted and brought up by childless fascist families. It has been proven that this happened on many thousands of occasions. It was still happening well into the 1980s. It is strange to think that among Franco apologists there may be some of those stolen babies, and they will never know that their biological parents were Republican supporters. Only now in the 2020s, are the Spanish people learning the full scale of these and other atrocities which were still secretly taking place after the transition to democracy.

Naturally Geordie was immensely downhearted and angry at Franco's victory but he still fought for his beliefs at home. He spent a long time recovering from the physical effects of his time in Spain and, due to being blacklisted, had enormous difficulty in finding long-term work. He did some odd labouring jobs when they turned up but that was not often enough. Times were hard and he had a growing family to keep.

Geordie was correct in his belief that if the fascists were not defeated in Spain, war would soon follow for his own country and many others.

As regards the men who fought against fascism in Spain, I have seen them wrongly compared with others who have more recently gone to fight in foreign conflicts. On the television programme *Question Time*, an audience member suggested that British citizens who were going to fight alongside Isis in the conflict in Syria were no different to those who went to Spain to join the International Brigade. No one on the panel contradicted that comment. They should have explained that those who travelled to Syria in support of religious fanatics had no interest in what the people of that country wanted, whereas the volunteers who went to Spain went to fight fascism, in support of a democratically elected government which was greatly improving the lives of working class people.

Many years ago, someone in Prestonpans was talking about British mercenaries who were in Africa at the time. He went on to say to me, 'just like your Dad did in Spain'. I let him know in no uncertain terms that there was no comparison between men fighting for the highest bidder, and the brave men who freely gave everything to defend the Spanish people from the fascists.

Just prior to the Second World War, one of the jobs he did get was as a concrete worker, helping in the building of the anti-tank concrete-block defences along the coast of East Lothian in the build-up to the war.

Second World War

By the start of the Second World War, Geordie and Ellen had five children to care for and during the war, Ellen worked at the Cockenzie boatyard to help provide for her family. Geordie served in the Royal Artillery. He served in Madagascar, India, Persia (now Iran), Iraq, Sicily, Gallipoli, North Africa and Egypt but, in later life he hardly mentioned the war. Perhaps he thought fascism should have been defeated long before that and didn't want to dwell on it.

Geordie occasionally talked about the times when, along with other like-minded men, he had arranged meetings among the troops to stress the need to open a second front in Europe. He believed that to have done so would have released pressure on the Soviet Union, which was suffering huge losses at that time. He recalled that, one time, when the troops were being given instructions on machine gun assembly, he was asked to assemble one and the instructor was amazed at how quickly he completed the task. Geordie explained that he had done it previously during the Spanish Civil War. The instructor said it was ridiculous that Geordie was listed as having no military experience. It would appear that to have fought in the Spanish Civil War was deemed irrelevant.

One thing I can say for certain is that I had never seen Dad lose his temper, so I was surprised at one event he did mention. I think he was in Persia, being drilled by a loud-mouthed sergeant. It was extremely hot and the men were all sweating. Geordie's rifle had slipped from his hand. The sergeant screamed at him, 'Watters have you never handled a rifle before?' Geordie snatched the rifle up and, with his finger on the trigger, pointed it at the sergeant and said, 'Yes, I have used a rifle before and it was to shoot better men than you.' Although he could have been in serious trouble, he never heard another word out of that sergeant, who probably felt lucky to escape with his life.

When I was about 13, I came across Geordie's WW2 discharge papers and to me it looked like he had a great report but, when I asked him where his medals were, he replied that you don't fight for medals. Geordie's war record states that he was:

A loyal and serious minded soldier of considerable experience. He understands the full meaning of the word team-work. He is of sober and very willing disposition.

I was not surprised at that, I would have expected no less.

After the war, Geordie still had difficulty in finding employment. He was still blacklisted from the mines because of his political activities and record of encouragement for the miners to strike. There was never anything available to Geordie. His problem was solved one day when he went to see the manager at Prestonlinks Colliery, where they had been advertising for workers. Having worked in the pits since he was a young lad, Geordie was an experienced miner but the management did not want men known as active trade unionists and, in their opinion, troublemakers. Geordie had recently received a letter from his comrade, Willie Gallacher, a popular Communist MP at the time. Without mentioning the letter, Geordie held it in his hand with the House of Commons emblem clearly showing. The manager had been indicating that he could not find work for him. Geordie, aware that the manager had noticed the letter, said to him, 'If there is no work for me this matter will have to go further.' His bluff paid off and he was finally back working as a miner. He was now able to provide for his family and worked in the mines till he reached retirement age.

He was elected as NUM chairman for that pit, a position he held till the pit closed 20 years later, he then went to work at Monktonhall Colliery. It was a common thing for local men to tell me that if they had a problem with their wages or bad treatment by management they would go to Geordie Watters, he was the man to get it sorted out. It is worth pointing out that at that time, as a union official, he had to work his full shift first then take care of any grievances the men had. This was unpaid work that meant every day in life he would be late getting home, but he never complained.

He had less success on the many occasions he stood as a Communist Party candidate in the council elections. There were three council positions in Prestonpans, always contested by three Communists and three Labour candidates. Geordie always got a lot more votes than any of the other Communist candidates, including one who had previously been a Labour councillor but had defected to the Communist Party. However, he never managed to get elected. Up until his final years, I frequently witnessed people saying to him that if only he had stood for another party, they would definitely have voted for him. He simply told them he was a communist and would be remaining a communist. That would never change.

He often spoke about his friend Willie Gallacher being asked how he felt about the constant criticism he received from the press. Willie replied that he found it reassuring, as it was an indication he was looking after his constituents. After 15 years as an MP, Gallacher lost his seat to Willie Hamilton, who had lied during the campaign, claiming that Gallacher had attended a royal garden party. Hamilton only admitted this wasn't true after winning the election, but he claimed he had been misinformed. Geordie had enormous respect for Gallacher and, along with my brother Jimmy, canvassed for him during election campaigns. Gallacher made several visits to our family home during the 1940s. He was one of Geordie's heroes, as was Lenin and several other communists. I rather like the fact that, far from hiding his beliefs, Dad was openly proud of them. As well as the family photo taken in 1937 and one of Uncle Willie in Spain, we had a portrait of Lenin above the living-room fireplace.

I was about seven years old when an older kid insultingly said to me, 'Your dad's a commie.' I had no idea what that was but it seemed to be a bad thing! As for Geordie being a communist, I am now in my 70s and, in my opinion, have yet to meet a better man.

One day in the early 1960s, I was out with a pal. As we passed the town hall, my pal ran over to look at a noticeboard which displayed the names of people who were in arrears with their rent. That public shaming of debtors was a real disgrace and I was disappointed that my friend took pleasure in it. Sometime after that, a group of five or six people arrived at our house to ask Geordie to help them as they were being evicted for rent arrears and they didn't have money to pay. They certainly didn't think Geordie had money to pay their arrears but they knew he had a history of helping people. What he did do was to go round various organisations asking them to make a contribution to save the soon-to-be-evicted tenants. Among those he asked for help were groups he certainly would not have been fond of, such as Toc H (Talbot House), a right-wing religious group. Despite his anger at the Catholic Church's collusion with Franco in Spain, Geordie also went to ask the local priest for assistance for these people. In the local chapel, the Catholics had been told that they must not vote for Geordie or any other communists in the council elections. In spite of that, Geordie often praised the fact that not only did the priest make a donation, he insisted on not being told if any of those being evicted were Catholic or not as he simply wanted to help.

By 1953, Geordie and Ellen had a family of eight: George, Ellen, Billy, Jimmy, Davie, Tam, Isabel and Mary. All went on to produce many grandchildren, every one of them extremely proud of both Ellen and Geordie.

Outside politics, Geordie had a wide range of interests. He liked the music of Paul Robeson, Tom Paxton, Pete Seeger and Ewan MacColl. He also enjoyed reading the works of Jack London, Robert Burns and Omar Khayyam. A favourite book of his was Thomas Johnston's *History of the Working Classes in Scotland*. In the mid 1960s when my future wife – who had absolutely no interest in, or knowledge of, politics – first visited my parents, Geordie gave her an old copy of Robert Tressell's *The Ragged Trousered Philanthropists*. To her, it seemed a strange gift but she politely accepted it. She then read it and was very impressed and moved by it, and she still recommends it to people today; it was her first introduction to politics.

Another of my father's interests was sport. He often spoke about how Jack Johnson, the first black boxer to be World Heavyweight Champion, was only the first one because other black boxers had been denied the chance to fight for the title. Another two sporting heroes of his were boxer Joe Lewis and tennis player Rod Laver.

In the 1960s he was still involved in protesting and demonstrating against political and social injustices. On one occasion two members of the CND's Committee of One Hundred stayed overnight at our house. In the morning, Geordie left with them to demonstrate against the Polaris submarines being deployed at Holy Loch. Later that evening, I heard my mother saying that my father had been arrested and put in a police cell, but I don't remember if he was ever charged or had to go to court. Strangely, at the time I didn't think that my father's detention was a significant enough event for any of the family to worry about!

I think that might have happened the same year our family went to Glasgow's St Andrew's Halls for Willie Gallacher's 80th birthday celebration on 24 December 1961. I was 14 and had no real interest in politics, but he made a big impression on me. I remember him talking about his concern about nuclear weapons with a sincerity that I will never forget. It was then that I understood my father's respect and great admiration for him.

Geordie was always an atheist but did not have a problem with others having religious beliefs. In his eyes, everyone was entitled to their own beliefs. He had many friends from different political backgrounds too but, not surprisingly, none of them were Tory supporters.

One thing Geordie and Ellen had no time for was royalty and they would happily have seen them removed from any position of influence. My older brother Jimmy and myself remember our parents reminiscing about a royal visit to this area. As usual with these events, a great fuss was being made and many houses in the neighbourhood had Union Jack flags on display. My parents spoke with great pride about the fact that they had hung a Soviet hammer and sickle flag from their window. I can imagine them doing that. We are not sure about the exact date of the event and I wish we had shown more interest when these things were being discussed.

When television channels played the National Anthem after their final broadcast of the day, my father would spring out of his chair and, with a few choice words, dash to find the Off switch! He could not bear to listen to that hated tune and what it signified.

Geordie was a teetotaller, only making an exception at New Year or on special occasions, when he would have a drink to be sociable. I remember in the 1960s his one small 'vice' was a few shillings a week spent in the bookie's shop round the corner; he meticulously checked the form of the horses in the *Daily Worker/Morning Star*. He never spent money he could not afford though, and always told me that he had never met a poor bookie, so it was unwise to gamble. Geordie was a very quietly spoken man who rarely lost his temper, but he did show some real annoyance when 'his' horse lost, which to be honest, was rather often! A treat for him and Ellen was a visit to the Powderhall Dog Track in Edinburgh.

I remember one day he had given a talk to the members of Edinburgh Young Communist League. One of them had a car and, along with two other YCL members, ran Geordie home. Seeing me, someone around their own age, they wanted to chat. They said they thought Geordie was a great man but they would not like to be his son. I don't know what he had said to them, but they thought he was a disciplinarian. This made me laugh. As a long-haired, unemployed young man in the early 1960s, I always got to do whatever I wanted and dressed the way I wanted. Dad never put any pressure on me to find a job. His only concern was for my welfare and the one time he did give unasked-for advice was when I had already decided I was going to work in the coal mines. He said that, going by his own personal experience, he did not agree with me doing that. However, I did go on to work in the mines. He never instigated political debate or put any pressure on me to adopt his views. My interest in political matters came from watching him and learning from him.

Geordie had been abroad when fighting in Spain and during the Second World War but had never been able to afford a holiday outside Britain. So, in 1977, the family paid for a short holiday for Geordie and Ellen in Leningrad in the Soviet Union, a dream come true for Geordie. The trip was deliberately timed for the 60th anniversary of the Russian Revolution. They had never imagined they would be able to travel abroad, so to visit the Soviet Union, the home of the Russian Revolution, was a real thrill for both of them. There was great excitement when they got their passports and went on their way. They

At the unveiling of a Spanish Civil War memorial plaque in Prestonpans, April 1978.
Top: Geordie Watters (L) with Tommy Bloomfield (R); bottom: with Jack Jones.

had a wonderful holiday and the experience left a big impression on Geordie.

In April 1978, a Spanish Civil War memorial plaque was unveiled in Prestonpans to commemorate the men who had lost their lives in that conflict, the two local men being Ellen's brother, Willie Dickson and their friend, Jock Gilmour. It was an excellent event for several reasons. Firstly, the plaque was unveiled by Jack Jones, a genuine socialist who had also fought in Spain and who was Britain's best-known trade union leader. A number of members of the International Brigade also attended, including Tom Murray, George Drever and Stevie Fullarton who, many years later, became Scotland's last surviving volunteer. For Geordie, the most important attendee at the event was his old comrade and friend, Tommy Bloomfield. It was great to see how much they enjoyed being in each other's company again.

In the Labour Club, where the reception was being held, I said to Tommy that it was really good of him to make the effort to travel to Prestonpans from Kirkcaldy for the event. Tommy replied that if he couldn't make the effort for Geordie Watters then he couldn't make it for anyone.

Willie Dickson's widow and family were there. And also, I imagine, Jock Gilmour's and Jimmy Kempton's relatives; I wish I had looked out for them that day and told them how much I admired their relatives.

The four men who went to Spain were all heroes. Geordie was the last surviving local man.

Jack Jones kindly signed the commemorative leaflet.

It was very fortunate that these events took place when they did, because the next year Geordie started to suffer from dementia and eventually the difficult decision was made for him to go into a care home, which was devastating for him and the family. The last time I visited him a nurse mentioned that he seemed even more confused than usual and had been talking about things that could never have happened. He had been telling them that he had been to Leningrad and he had gone into great detail about the trip. It was still a very unusual holiday destination at that time, especially in a small community like Prestonpans, and the nurses had put his story down to his dementia. They were rather surprised to find out that his story had been true. But, for the family, it was comforting to think that in spite of his dreadful illness he was able to remember that holiday and had some happy memories of it during that awful time in hospital. He died shortly after that.

The year after Geordie died, politician and trade unionist Jimmy Reid unveiled a bench in Tower Gardens, Prestonpans to commemorate the men of the International Brigades. That event was attended by, among others, Willie Dickson's widow, Margaret, several International Brigade members, including Stevie Fullarton, and local councillors. I was proud to be asked to carry the IB banner to represent Geordie. Sadly, the bench has since been vandalised and removed, and the plaque from it is missing.

In 2006, Geordie's family were invited to a Civic Reception for Umberto Sereni, Mayor of Barga, whose hometown in Italy is twinned with Prestonpans. Before the reception, he placed a wreath beside the International Brigades' memorial plaque at Prestonpans Civic Square. He was delighted to meet us as his father, an Italian, had also been in the International Brigades. That was an extremely dangerous and brave thing to do when his own country was fighting in support of the fascists. The Mayor told us that he had written a book about his father's experiences in Spain.

In 2015, Wonder Fools, a young Scottish theatre group, got in touch to tell us that they were working on a play based on the story of the four local men who had travelled to Spain to fight fascism. The theatre group wanted to talk to the relatives of the men to get an idea of the men's characters. The writers were Jack Nurse and Robbie Gordon. Robbie is the grandson of Pat O'Brien, an ex-councillor and former Provost of East Lothian. Pat had been involved in getting the Spanish Civil War memorial plaque put up in Prestonpans. He had told Robbie the story of the men, and that gave them the idea for *549: Scots of the Spanish Civil War*.

During 2018 and 2019, with a wonderful group of actors and Jack Nurse doing an excellent job as producer, the play had two sell-out tours throughout Scotland and as far as London. These performances were so successful that, in 2022, Wonder Fools received funding for a new tour of the play.

Prestonpans Town Hall was packed with family members of the four men, especially in the first days of the performances. It was a very emotional experience for everyone from these families but even people who were not related in any way to the men were moved to tears. When I spoke to some of the actors and congratulated them on their success, they said it had been a privilege to play the characters of Geordie and his friends and family.

About a year before the first theatre performances, Wonder Fools had a preliminary reading of the script in Prestonpans Labour Club. Afterwards, I spoke to one of Uncle Willie's family, who said they had always been led to believe that Willie had sacrificed his life for nothing. However, after attending the reading, they understood his reasons for going to Spain to fight, and now realised it had indeed been a very worthwhile cause.

I had never done any research into my father's activities in the Spanish Civil War, probably because he seldom spoke about it much himself and, as children, we just took it for granted that it had been a normal thing for any man to do. However, a few years ago my daughter Angela came across the Scotland and the Spanish Civil War Facebook page and advised me to have a look. I was very impressed by it and started to research more sites and was amazed at the amount of information available. My son Steven found a reference to my father on the Marx Memorial Library website and I sent an email to them explaining my interest in the item. In response I received a wonderful memento of my parents.

Apparently, back in 1937 after Mum had seen the cinema newsreel and a newspaper article about the prisoners, she wrote to what appears to be the International Brigades Dependants' Aid Committee, telling them that although she had received no official confirmation about Geordie's welfare, she now knew for sure that he was still alive. The letter and a copy of the newspaper photo were in the files of the Marx Memorial Library, and they sent me copies. I could not believe how lucky I was to get that picture that day as up till then I had never seen any photos of Dad when he was a young man, other than the one that had been made while he was missing during the Spanish Civil War – and, as I was not born until 1947, my earliest memories of him are of a man in his 50s. By that time, after having had a rather hard life he had changed considerably.

The *Daily Mail* article shows what side they supported, with their description of the men as 'Reds' awaiting food rations. Under another photo in the same paper they described the men as 'misguided and hapless British prisoners' who, they claimed, were sent out to Spain by Communists with promises of £6 a week, and the first they knew of their fate was when they were handed arms and sent to the front. It was the *Daily Mail* that was misguided. Contrary to the newspaper's claims, the men were well aware of the dangers of fascism and what they were fighting for in Spain.

On the copy of the picture which Mum had sent she indicated Geordie by marking an X on the plate that he held.

The letter Mum sent on 14 April 1937 says she hopes that if the photo was published in the *Daily Worker* it might help ease the minds of relatives of other prisoners. Notice she begins with 'Dear Comrade' and ends with

Daily Mail, 31 March 1937.

'Yours Fraternally'. Mum was a member of the Communist Party too.

On the same day that the photo and letter arrived I received an email from Willy Maley, whose father was one of Dad's fellow prisoners. He told me that his father was in a scene in the RTÉ documentary film *Even the Olives are Bleeding.* I then had the surprise of discovering that the clip was from what had originally been the Pathé newsreel of British prisoners who were

Gallacher   Box 50/Wa/1

5 Grange Rd
Prestonpans
East Lothian
15·4·37.

Dear Comrade

I have had no farther word from you since the letter stating that my husband was missing so I take it that you dont know my husband is one of Franko's prisoners. This is a photo taken out of the mail he is Third in the row and I have also seen him in the news reel in the pictures there is no mistaken him as he comes right to the front Well comrade if this photo was put in the daily it might help some other comrade to pick out there relatives and ease someones mind as it has done mine and comrade in case you think I am mading a mistake show this photo to com Gallicor as he knew my husband and could I have the photo back as I would like to keep it

yrs t'val.

Mrs. George Watters

Letter sent by Ellen Watters on 15 April 1937 after seeing a newsreel showing her husband as a prisoner in Spain. (Reproduced courtesy of the Marx Memorial Library)

being held in Spain. So, because I now knew what Dad looked like as a young man from the newly discovered photo, I was able to recognise him in that scene too. I had seen that documentary a couple of times before but, as it is predominantly about the Irish International Brigaders, I did not realise that this particular clip was actually of my father and his comrades when they were filmed at the prison in 1937. The images were not very clear but Jimmy Maley and my dad were both visible. That was one of the most emotional days of my life. I watched that clip over and over again. To see my father standing there in that hell-hole, not knowing whether or not he would ever see his loved ones again, was, to say the least, emotional in the extreme. A few years later, we found the original Pathé News Archives clip and also one made when the men were being released. These images are much clearer and it still makes me feel emotional when I watch it. We were aware that there was footage of these events but, after many years of searching, we had given up hope of ever finding it. I wish my mother and father could have seen it.

```
Reference:              C.I. CARD.

Name:                   WATTERS, George.

Address:                5, Grange Road, Preston Pans,
                        Scotland.

Date of birth:          26.9.04. Preston Pans.

Occupation:             Miner.

General history:  25.4.29.  Communist(intercept.)
7.11.31.  Communist candidate for Preston Pans Municipal
Election - unsuccessful. 7.11.32.  Spoke at a N.U.WM.
meeting of his experiences during Hunger March to London
(E'burgh Police Rep:) 17.4.34. Sec: of Preston Pans branch
of N.U.WM. (intercept.) 20.12.36.  Leftfor Spain.(S.B. rep:
no ref.) 30.5.37.  Released by Franco, having been taken
prisoner, and repatriated to U.K. (SB. rep. no ref.)
```

Geordie Watters' MI5 card.

Of course, all the men taking part in the Spanish Civil War were being monitored by MI5 and after making some enquiries I was sent a copy of Dad's MI5 card.

I'm also pleased to own the Spanish Civil War badge which my Dad always wore.

Geordie was very proud to have been a member of the No. 2 Machine Gun Company of the British Battalion of the XV International Brigade, a Company of very brave individuals. In 2021, Prestonpans Labour Club installed a stained-glass window to honour the four local men who had gone to Spain. All four men's names are engraved on it.

La Pasionaria's famous words about the International Brigades were: 'You are history. You are legend'. A fitting tribute to each and every one of them.

For me, one of the most poignant moments in 549 was when the actress who played my mother stood up in the cinema and, on seeing Geordie on the screen, cried out, 'That's him, that's my Geordie!' The cast of the play portrayed that moment beautifully and the emotions felt in the hall were very real. It was amazing imagining how my mother had felt on seeing at last that her husband was still alive.

Geordie was a small man but had the heart of a lion and I am proud to have had him as my father.

There's a valley in Spain called Jarama
  It's a place that we all know so well
  It is there that we gave of our manhood
  And so many of our brave comrades fell
  We are proud of the British Battalion
  And the stand for Madrid that they made
  For they fought like true sons of the soil
  As part of the Fifteenth Brigade.

  So comrades come rally,
  And the last fight let us face,
  The Internationale unites the human race.

4

ARCHIBALD CAMPBELL McASKILL WILLIAMS
'Rosemary for remembrance – is he still alive?'

Lisa Croft

MY GRANDFATHER NEVER talked to his daughters and grandchildren about his involvement in the Spanish Civil War. After he died my grandmother, Jane Orme, mentioned it in passing and I regret not discussing it further. It was only when I started to research my family history that I found out aspects of his life through documents and newspaper articles. My mum Rosemary and her sister Jennifer knew very little. Amazingly about 15 years ago some of his papers were discovered in a suitcase in Jen's Los Angeles garden summer house, including a small notebook, sketches and notes from his time in Spain. Around this time, I was contacted by Alan Lloyd, a member of the International Brigade Memorial Trust (IBMT), who sent me MI5 documents from the National Archives at Kew and information from the Marx Memorial Library which really filled in the gaps. Michael Harrison, a Toronto local historian, provided me with newspaper articles about my grandfather's time in two Canadian prisons during the 1920s and 1930s.

My mum and I became fascinated with all aspects of the Spanish Civil War and visited the People's History Museum in Manchester where the IBMT had an exhibition of photographs and information. We met Dolores and Hilary, the daughters of Manchester volunteer Sam Wild, and we joined the IBMT. Mum and I attended as many lectures and exhibitions as possible. We also visited Madrid and Jarama on their annual commemorative event.

I joined local groups across the north-west, meeting others with a similar interest, including Stuart Walsh and Terry Bayes, volunteer archivists at the Working Class Movement Library in Salford, who are collecting and digitalising hundreds of Spanish Civil War documents and photographs.

I became involved in setting up new memorials in my area, in Wigan and Bolton, and an exhibition and talk in Adlington about the Spanish Republican internment camp situated there after the war. Currently I am pushing for a plaque at the Watermillock, Bolton, a large stately home that gave refuge to many Basque children.

Discovering about my grandfather has been a rewarding and emotional experience for mum and me.

Archibald Campbell McAskill Williams, known as AC, and sometimes Archie, was a working man, self-educated and intelligent, well informed through his life experiences. His mixed accent told the tale of his travels – traces of southern Hampshire English and a Highland Scots lilt, with a dominant North American drawl.

He experienced the loss of his family when he emigrated to Canada in 1923. He worked for low pay with thousands of other unemployed men. Competing for work during the 'depression years' in Canada led him to suffer victimisation and hostility. These experiences shaped the lifelong socialist convictions and principles which would see him meet his wife Jane Orme, join the International Brigades and travel to fight in the Spanish Civil War in late 1936. He was a warm, kind and principled man. He was my grandfather.

AC aged 19, second left with brothers Donald, Peter and Finlay before he sets sail to Canada.

Politicisation

AC was born to Scottish parents at 90, Percy Road, Southsea, Portsmouth on 3 October 1904, the first of six sons; his brothers were Donald, Peter, Finlay, Alex and Angus. His father, John, had migrated to work in the HM shipyards on the south coast in the 1890s after his apprenticeship in Greenock. His mother, Julia McAskill was from a family of tenant crofters from the hamlet of Greep on the Isle of Skye.

When AC was about ten years old, the family moved for his father to work in another Royal Navy dockyard at Invergordon on the Cromarty Firth, north of Inverness, where there was a famous naval mutiny in 1931. During the First World War the town's population had mushroomed and the Williams family were just some of the 6,000 people who moved there for work in the dockyards.

As a child, AC was a very bright pupil. Excelling in Mathematics, he obtained a scholarship to study at Invergordon Academy. When he left school, the Williams family moved again. This time his father's work took him to Leith dockyards and the family lived in a tenement flat at 7 Melgund Terrace, Edinburgh.

AC's first job was as an insurance clerk on low pay. Opportunities for an educated young man were limited and when a sponsorship opportunity arose to travel across the Atlantic and take up secure employment and training as a bank clerk at the Dominion Bank in Brantford near Toronto, Canada, he took it. In 1923, aged 19, AC sailed from Glasgow aboard *The Marloch* bound for St. John, New Brunswick. The pain and sorrow at leaving his country, home and family was immense. Little did he know that this would be the very last time that he would see his mother and father.

AC took lodgings at 94 Superior Street, Brantford, Ontario. In his new position as a front-of-house cash clerk in the Dominion Bank, he was keen to impress his employers. He did not drink or gamble. His passion was dancing and he attended popular local dance halls, becoming a cool and stylish mover in Charleston and jazz styles. These were precursors of the New York Lindy Hop which he mastered some years later. AC explored Toronto on his days off. His new and exciting experiences in Canada were far removed from his previous restricted lifestyle in distant Edinburgh. He sent home money every month, helping to support his parents and younger brothers.

His parents retired and moved back to live at Hallin on the Waternish Peninsula of Skye, north of Dunvegan near to where Julia was born. She was happy to be in the company of her sisters Maggie and Mary again and the couple lived there for the rest of their days.

After three years in the bank, AC was experiencing the life of a young, single man with good prospects, when a dramatic incident occurred which meant his new dream lifestyle was all to go terribly wrong. Due to a faulty electric cable, a fire started in the public hall of the Dominion Bank. The senior teller had $20,000 in the 'cage' at his till and on the sound of the alarm, rushed to place some of it in the fireproof safe, but was overcome with fumes, fainting on the steps to the vaults. Without thinking of his own safety, AC picked up his colleague and carried him through the thick smoke to safety, then dashed back into the building again to collect the money which was scattered over the floor, carrying it to the Commercial Bank across the street. He returned a third time and found an overlooked $500 on the floor and, overcome by temptation, he quickly hid it for himself, to recover later.

This large sum of cash amounted to a year's salary and a few days after the commotion of the fire, AC applied for a post thousands of miles away in California, this job offering a much higher rate of pay at $35 a week. With part of the hidden, and now stolen, Dominion Bank money, he bought a ticket plus two suits and two pairs of shoes. This outlay led to suspicion and under pressure of interrogation by bank officials, he broke down and told them the truth. The police were called and he was arrested. At his trial his counsel pled for lenient treatment due to AC's previous good character and asked for his brave actions during the fire to be taken into account. But the judge and jury failed to agree and to his shock, AC was sentenced to two years in prison. Letters of support in the local newspaper highlighting the disgraceful salaries that banks paid their junior employees, included a fellow bank teller who signed himself 'One of the sufferers'. He wrote:

> It's about time the bank tellers of Canada were getting salaries in keeping with their responsibilities while the profits of the banks were counted in millions.

This devastating event not only gave AC a criminal record but he lost his job and also his home. Worst of all was the fact that his employers wrote to his family in Scotland. His mother was so disappointed, ashamed and furious with her eldest son that she never had any contact with him again. After AC had served his time it was arranged that he be deported. Somehow he managed to evade the authorities and make a run for it. He chose to take his chances, homeless and unemployed, rather than return to an unwelcoming family in Scotland.

Now aged 23, he took to the road, taking whatever work he could get. He cut corn in the boiling heat of Kansas, and worked as a rancher in Virginia – a real cowboy! He'd also been a fur trapper in the Canadian wilds of Saskatchewan, and knew how to skin animals and cure their skins. He once came face to face with a grizzly bear that had approached the forest camp. His friend had no choice but to shoot it between the eyes at point-blank range, saving both their lives.

AC became a husky-dog-team driver in Alaska, transporting fur and meat across vast icy expanses. He'd worked as a Lumberjack and gave the family vivid accounts of riding logs down rivers. Explaining how a tree is made to fall in the right place, he mentioned that one of his friends miscalculated and died under a falling tree. Along the way AC 'panned' for gold, gambled in card games for money and got into fights with anyone who was cheating. His varied employment and adventures must have been amazing for a young man, yet for many years, he had to block out the sadness of estrangement from his parents and brothers and fend off his desperate loneliness.

During the 'Great Depression' in North America, work dried up. AC found himself in the company of thousands of other unemployed men, often young immigrants like himself, faced with the difficult task of finding work; but close friendships were soon forged with others in his predicament. Federal government officials estimated that in the late 1920s at least 70,000 'single homeless unemployed males' were travelling about the country in search of work. Thousands of immigrants, who faced widespread prejudice and victimisation, were deported to their original home-lands. Some went voluntarily, disillusioned by Canada's 'promised land'.

Meeting up with new comrades in similar situations, AC walked for miles looking for work. Often, for free travel, they 'rode the rods' – a dangerous practice of riding illegally in or on top of a box car freight train. Local authorities often actively encouraged this to keep the unemployed 'army' on the move and makeshift shelters housing hundreds of men grew up alongside the tracks.

AC talked about his time on the road as if it was full of excitement and adventure, choosing to play down hunger and exhaustion. He was arrested on a few occasions for vagrancy and gave the alias of William Johnson. (He was John's son and a Williams!)

Prejudice and victimisation were common practice by government officials, with the excuse of reducing relief costs in local government. The Canadian Department of Immigration moved to a new phase of deportation work. It advocated that deportations could take place for anyone attempting to create a riot or public disorder. Communist immigrants were targeted for unlawful assembly or striking, but political activity in the form of demonstrations increased with large numbers of organised unemployed swelling the ranks.

Many were deported to their home countries; in those governed by military regimes, some of these so-called radicals were executed on arrival.

Examples of strikers or 'radicals' include Askell Panjata, who was arrested for marching in a parade of unemployed workers, jailed for three months and deported to Finland despite protests that his life would be in serious danger; another was Jewish radical Hymie Sparaga, arrested while on a picket line of garment workers, deported shortly afterwards to Germany and later killed by the Nazis.

Directed by the local authorities, law and order was enforced by the Royal Canadian Mounted Police, the Mounties, who harassed the organised unemployed on a continual basis. Peaceful outdoor rallies were often dispersed in a violent manner yet right-wing vigilante groups were often supported and in 1929 in Saskatchewan, the Ku Klux Klan helped to elect a sympathetic candidate in the Province.

Work camps were established throughout Canada, the authorities making it compulsory for unemployed men to take residence. The presence of single, transient unemployed people in large numbers was feared by the authorities and rather than be denied relief or face arrest for vagrancy many were forced into these camps. AC was one of them.

The camp administrators were very strict and 'inmates' were denied many basic civil rights, while at the same time they were not permitted to complain about the harsh regime. They were expected to work eight-hours-a-day hard labour, such as making roads, in exchange for poor-quality food, lodging in bunk rooms that were generally filthy, plus a pitiful, insulting allowance of 20 cents a day.

A large militia camp was erected by the Department of National Defence

(DND) at Dundurn outside Saskatoon in the state of Saskatchewan. It was built by the local conservative government as a response to overcrowding and unrest at a camp nearby, AC was one of the residents.

He was the leader and spokesperson of the Saskatoon relief camp delegations during the spring of 1933. Many delegations reported to the authorities regarding conditions in the camp and some small improvements had been implemented. A large number of political inmates were identified to take residence in the new military-run camp, including those who were seen as agitators.

Tensions were high on 8 May 1933 at the annual May Day Parade at the Saskatoon Melee exhibition ground. The event was in full swing and citizens were joined by the unemployed relief camp inmates plus huge numbers of mounted police. Things soon became heated and there were angry scenes. A mounted police charge provoked a riot with many injured. Inspector Lorne Sampson fell from his horse and struck his head on an iron post. He died from his injuries. Twenty-six rioters were arrested and taken into custody in Saskatoon police station and a few days later were transferred to Prince Albert Jail. Due to the large numbers, a makeshift prison vehicle was used – a furniture van. The inmates sang 'The Red Flag' on top note as the van rolled on the route. Hundreds of sightseers came to see the prisoners escorted by four prison guards in red tunics followed by an automobile full of more uniformed men. The next day, local newspaper *Star and Phoenix* stated that they were searching for their leader, 29-year-old British immigrant, Archibald Campbell Williams, who had evaded arrest – at the demonstration he had been one of the main speakers. But he was easily found at the camp and arrested. Officers discovered a minute book used to record meetings, which they took as evidence. All of those arrested were later tried and imprisoned for unlawful assembly and rioting.

AC's trial came after 87 days on remand separated from his comrades. He applied through his counsel, Mr Newlove, for permission to represent himself. His counsel stated that the prisoner was not only his client but his friend. Before a gallery of spectators, including some 15 Saskatoon barristers, AC made his uninterrupted address for 55 minutes with calm and restraint. He proceeded to give his picture of relief camp conditions which were deplorable, men living amidst filth in a stifling atmosphere in which cooking, toilet and other smells combined. He claimed that the few improvements made by camp officials were due to the organised

The Star-Phoenix Goes Home

Williams Blames Police Head For Trouble At Camp

AC's trial reported in the local press.

pressure of the men. He described the aggressive treatment of agitators by the police, stating that agitating is not wrong so long as the object was worthy and that during his stay he had found many worthy objects to agitate for. He reviewed at length the Crown evidence conclusions of the disturbance, maintaining that officers had contradicted themselves many times as to what actually happened. He blamed Chief Donald, the main Crown witness, whose dramatic account of events became the evidence responsible for the conviction of other camp inmates. He asserted that Chief Donald could have prevented the riot and was in fact regarded by many people in Saskatoon as the real cause of the violence. In AC's closing speech to the jury, he pointed out that many jurymen have sons growing up who might someday be in the same position as relief camp inmates. If unemployed, they too might attempt to secure improvements in their conditions and that was the only crime he had committed. He added that he would be prepared to do the same thing again.

AC's two defence witnesses, Walter James Rockhill and Jack McEwan, both fellow camp inmates, gave their version of events and conditions. The two men were to be transferred along with AC to the new Regina camp but all were unwilling to go. Rockhill stated that AC had urged the men not to resort to violence. Although AC gave a wonderful and positive case in court for himself and his comrades, and despite having a supportive counsel, it was all to no avail. This was due to the hammer blow against AC when the court was informed of his previous conviction for stealing $500 from the Dominion Bank and the information that he had been meant to be deported in March 1926 and was therefore an illegal alien. Mr Justice Embury pronounced the verdict for AC as guilty. He was imprisoned for unlawful assembly and rioting with hard labour, a sentence of two years, less the 87 days already spent awaiting bail.

AC was released from jail in December 1935, aged 31; he was briefly reunited with his comrades until he was tracked down by the authorities. This time he really was deported and travelled back across the Atlantic in chains, having last been on British soil as a naïve optimistic teenager some 12 years earlier.

He arrived at Liverpool docks in December 1935. The north of England was not the best place to search for work. Unemployment was high.

Probably because his family had shunned him following his original prison sentence, he decided against returning to Scotland and headed for London, where he arrived demoralised and exhausted. He had heard there were places where men in his situation could get a decent meal and a clean bed for the night, even some clothing suitable for a damp British winter.

He made his way to the East End and on Christmas Eve he made his way to a recommended cafe without realising that this would be a life-changing decision.

Here he met Jane Orme Fetherstonhaugh, an erudite and articulate woman with an upper-class English accent and a friendly and capable manner. The secretary of the local National Unemployed Workers Movement (NUWM), she also assisted in the café. The attraction was mutual and they talked excitedly of Toronto, where she was born. Both recounted their championing of the underdog and discussed their dreams for a fairer society and the eradication of the injustice and economic inequality that afflicted the hungry poor. They were both members of the Communist Party.

Their friendship quickly developed into passion and a deeper love than they had ever known. Jane Orme's mother lent them the money to get married, so they rented a house in Trebarwith near Tintagel, Cornwall. On 23 March 1936, they tied the knot in the Registry Office in Camelford, his occupation stated as 'fur trapper' (his last employment) and they honeymooned at the ancient fishing village of Polperro.

Although with no money, no work and no secure home, their love was strong enough to keep their hopes high, but Jane Orme was pregnant and AC needed work. Throughout the late summer to autumn, AC continued his desperate quest for employment, staying at lodging houses along the south coast of England while Jane Orme stayed with her aunt in Cheltenham. On his travels, AC witnessed meetings of Mosley's British Union of Fascists, the Blackshirts, and wrote to his wife almost daily, describing the tension and mood of the people around him:

I saw a nice sign at the Dockers Meeting – SMASH FASCISM...

TAKE ACTION was scrawled on a wall near the docks...

The first boat I saw at the docks was the *Bremen* with the Swastika flying! That was an awful way to start the day.

The British Union of Fascists had rallies at places throughout the country, often trying to gain support amongst the large groups of unemployed men who gathered around places like the docks, looking for work. AC writes:

> I had an episode on Sunday night; I went up to hear the Blackshirts, damn them! But at least I found a *Daily Worker* from the opposition there!

News reports announced that a civil war had broken out in Spain. The ordinary people, many of them rural peasants, were opposing the bullying fascists, standing up to fight against them. In Britain, mainly amongst the left, there was widespread sympathy for the Spanish people.

AC wrote to Jane Orme, raising his concerns at what he was witnessing:

> I was muttering to myself after I had seen that Swastika flag and I saw a sign for the Consulado de España [Spanish Consulate]. The news from Spain did not sound so good.

The British Government decided not to get involved in the Spanish Civil War, declaring a non-intervention policy. If it had known what was to happen a few years later in 1939 when Hitler's Germany was to go to war with Britain and its allies, they might instead have decided to support the underdogs in Spain.

An 'Aid Spain' movement developed in many British towns. Thousands organised and contributed, helping to collect food, medical supplies and money for the Spanish people, who were short of just about everything. People from all around the world responded to the pleas from the Spanish Republican government and volunteered to fight on their side against Franco and his supporters, and the International Brigades were established.

By December 1936, after many months of searching, AC was still without work, income or security. Although Jane Orme was five months pregnant at the time, they agreed that there was only one course of action they could take.

Jane Orme had been to Spain in 1932 with her previous partner, fellow communist and trade union activist Julius Jacobs. Her mother had financed their plan and they hired a crew and a three-masted schooner, *The Three Sarahs*. The interesting group that sailed to Spain included Julius and Jane Orme, her mother Mimi and two young boys; 4-year-old Patrick, Jane Orme's son and 11-year-old John, her young brother. The group's intention was to distribute Marxist literature and their boat was seized in San Sebastián. All on board were arrested for a short time but the ship was impounded, never to be returned to the British owners, and the crew and family returned to London.

Since then Jane Orme had continued to be passionate about the Spanish Republican cause and she and AC made a decision. She would stay with friends in Portsmouth and AC would go to fight in Spain.

Spain

In November 1936, AC contacted the Communist Party in Portsmouth and volunteered to join the International Brigade. He was responsible for recruiting another member, Alexander Allen Foote, who was later to become one of the most notorious spies of the Second World War. AC left Jane Orme in Upper Arundel Street in Portsmouth, and he and Foote joined other volunteers travelling to Communist Party Headquarters in King Street, London to be briefed before setting off to Dover on 23 December 1936.

At the port they were met by police and MI5 representatives, who were on the lookout for men in large groups. Names of those suspected of travelling to Spain were taken and put on file at Whitehall.

On arrival at Gare du Nord in Paris, AC's group was met and taken to a secret location where they had a medical examination and awaited further instructions. The second stage of their journey took them by train to Perpignan, not far from the Spanish border where they were met by a coach that took them over the border on Christmas Day to Figueras. Soon after he arrived in Spain, AC became very ill with a fever and was escorted to Barcelona Military Hospital, where the wards were full of wounded people from Majorca.

Ten days later he was back with his group, the volunteers at the International Brigade headquarters at Albacete. He then joined the British Battalion based at Villarubia in Madrigueras as a member of the No.2 Machine Gun Company. AC had experience of firearms from when he worked as a fur trapper and rancher in North America. He complained that the firearm he had been issued was dangerous – it was old and it backfired. It looks as if he and the others were lucky to survive the training! At least three of AC's fellow prison and work-camp inmates who had taken part in the riot at Saskatoon were also International Brigade volunteers, including his friend Patrick O'Daire. Many other unemployed Canadians and immigrants joined

A letter home from Spain to Jane Orme.

the Mac-Pap Battalion (Mackenzie-Papineau), named after the leaders of the 1837–38 rebellions in upper and lower Canada.

On 6 February 1937, the newly formed 15th International Brigade Battalions, including AC's No. 2 Machine Gun Company, set off for the front to counter a new fascist offensive aimed at trying to cut off the road through the Jarama Valley that led to the Spanish capital, Madrid, which was held at that point by the Republican troops. Thousands of fascist troops were reported to be part of this operation, including the Army of Africa, known as the 'Moors', who were notorious for their brutality. AC's Company, led by Captain Harold Fry, was to cover the Brigade from sudden attack. During the battle there was heavy bombardment, causing huge loss of life on both sides. Tragically on the first day of fighting, half of the British Battalion were killed or wounded. The front continued to be held, despite their ancient guns having the wrong type of ammunition, but Fry's men were left isolated and freezing throughout the night. They were unaware that a Moorish unit had moved in close by. In the early hours, the Moors advanced. The Company were overpowered and captured.

Imprisoned In Franco's Jail

By the end of the Battle of Jarama, the Republicans had at least 10,000 dead or wounded and the Nationalists 6,000. Thirty members of the Machine Gun Company were captured. Nervous guards singled out a few comrades and they were shot in full view of the others. Twenty-seven of the Company's prisoners remained, including AC, and following these brutal scenes they too were lined up before a firing squad, only to be reprieved by a German officer who had spoken with the Spanish officer in charge of the execution and ordered the rifles to be lowered. To begin with the men had been mistaken for Russians, but the German officer realised that they were 'Inglés'. If it hadn't been for him, they would all have been shot. They were taken to San Martin Barracks, where they were told by a priest that they would be shot in the morning. But this did not happen. Instead they were taken by a lorry to Talavera de la Reina, an old pottery factory south of Madrid that was being used as a makeshift prison. A photograph taken when they were on the lorry was published in the right-wing newspaper the *Daily Mail*, with an article that cast the International Brigaders to be naïve fools.

In Talavera they were given heavy work repairing roads and digging graves to bury the bodies of executed Republican prisoners. The conditions were almost unbearable. They were very hungry and their only food was occasional helpings of beans. The Moorish guards had stolen their warm overcoats; in the freezing night they had to huddle together for warmth. Washing and toilet arrangements were dreadful as there was no clean water and those who were wounded lay unattended. Many fell ill. Their hair was shaved and they were covered in lice. They were beaten by guards and psychological fear haunted their days as they were under constant threat that they would be shot the next day, or the day after. Despite these squalid conditions and the brutality of the prison guards, the International Brigaders were the lucky ones as 30 other prisoners were shot every day, Spanish Republican prisoners being treated the worst of all.

At the end of March 1937, AC and his colleagues were paraded again in front of the world's press; this time a film crew made a newsreel of them being given cigarettes and food by prison officers, to show how 'reasonably' they were being treated. It was all a propaganda stunt – the cigarettes were taken back after filming. The film was shown around the world, including in UK cinemas. By chance, AC's mother-in-law, Mimi, saw it in Cheltenham while staying with her sister Olivia. She rushed to send a telegram to her daughter to tell her the exciting news that AC was still alive.

AC was unaware that his wife had given birth to a daughter on 23 March 1937, exactly a year to the day after they were married in Cornwall. Jane Orme, who heard nothing for months after hearing of the newsreel of his capture, presumed she was a widow and that the new father had died in a Spanish jail. She named her daughter Rosemary (for remembrance) and Nina ('girl' in Spanish). The thought of his wife and child must have kept AC going whilst in that prison cell, with all of the horrors he witnessed, trying to stay positive and to think of their future together.

AC kept a few notebooks hidden in his clothing, which still survive. Some of the pages refer to the names of his fellow prisoners, their ailments and their signatures. There are descriptions of a baseball game they'd organised in the prison grounds, including a score sheet and a match commentary. There are many handwritten pages of Spanish phrases with translations in English. This notebook must have been hidden very well, as any fellow Spanish prisoners assisting in such practices would have been shot. In one notebook there is a map of an unidentified prison. There is also a note written by a fellow prisoner, a Russian pilot and fellow prisoner, explaining his predicament. Translated in very basic English it mentions:

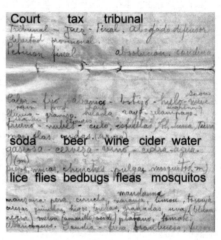

Notes on Spanish language made in one of AC Williams' hidden notebooks.

Anekcattgo Arekcustgrober Urykael (name?) mechanic shot down in 4/12 aircraft
Ju Opuxec-annapsium Epuinda (name?)
Soldier names Ekob (Ceyiarek) Hukorasbur aircraft T/UD
Tropuxoc annifam Gpumba
Pilots name Kputtiano-neuom.
He was imprisoned (In place?) Caia Manica?
Why do they exchange soldiers but not pilots. Names of aircraft taken to Germany 21 April 1934, Nobody knows where.

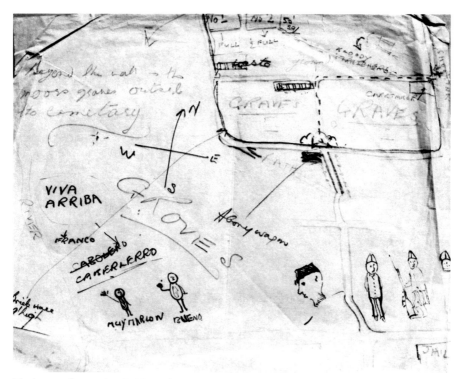

The layout of an unidentified Spanish prison where he was held as a POW sketched by AC Williams.

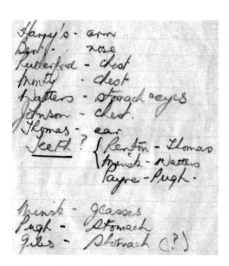

A page from one of AC Williams' hidden notebooks listing injuries and ailments of his fellow prisoners.

After being held at Talavera, AC and his comrades were transferred to a prison in Salamanca in an old monastery called Monasterio de la Caridad, a building that was used as a concentration camp during and after the war. On the day of their arrival, 37 Spanish Republicans had been shot dead, plus German and Russian International Brigade members. On arrival, they were each interrogated separately for one hour by Don Pablo Merry del Val, a Spanish fascist who stated that he was a lawyer. Del Val, who had been educated at Cambridge University and spoke very good English, acted as an official interpreter for Franco. In each interrogation, the same questions were asked, the answers were written down and signed by the prisoners. Prior to the interrogations, they had discussed how they would act and agreed to be vague and non-committal in their answers. Below is a transcript of the interrogation: (source MML Box 28/A/4) The actual document is faint and difficult to read.

This statement of AC 'Archie' Williams taken by Don Pablo Merry del Val acting as official interpreter of the government of Franco hereby interrogate the aforesaid who states: His name – his age – his political affiliation (none) member of T.U. (none)

Why did you come to Spain?
For work

How did you come to this country for work?
A man told me there was much work in Spain.

Who was this man?
Not sure. His name was Patterson or Patterman.

Where did you meet him?
Outside the Labour Exchange in Portsmouth.

You have been unemployed?
Yes

What did he say?
That if I wanted a job I could get lots of work in Spain.

Didn't you know there was a war on in Spain?
Yes but like all England thought it was only a small affair.

What happened next?
I accepted his offer.

And then?
We went to London together.

Who paid?
He paid for my ticket.

What happened then?
He asked me to wait in Victoria Station.

Yes and next?
I waited for an hour and he came back with two tickets to Paris.

Where did he get them?
I don't know.

Now listen Williams, I've two statements before yours and I know you fellows, all of you have had lots of time to think this over and from what we have in Navalcarnero we know you all came through King St. Did you?
I cannot say but some of the chaps did go, I suppose he went there too.

What happened next?
We went to Paris.

How?
Via Dunkirk

How?
Day excursion ticket.

Yes and next?
We arrived in Paris.

Where did you go?
I don't know Paris it was strange

[Refers to a file of papers] Place de Combat, a small street off it, CGT offices, is that right?
I don't know, it was Place something or other.

What happened next?
I waited outside and Patterson came back and gave me a meal ticket and went with me to a restaurant.

Where?
I don't know.

Name?
I don't know.

[Consults papers again, then gave name of café and address] Is that the place?
I don't know

And then?
We had our meal in company of about 30 others.

And then?
Patterson explained to me that I should go upstairs and wait till he returned.

And next?
I went upstairs and found these men who were also going to Spain.

And then?
We were taken to the station.

What station?
The Gare du Nord

Yes. Then?
We got on the train and got off at Perpignan.

Where was Patterson?
I don't know, I didn't see him again.

Were you surprised?
Yes, I thought he was coming along with me.

Ha! That's the way these Communists work, well what next?
We had a meal in Perpignan and crossed the border.

No. before that? You had an examination?
No.

Didn't you think that peculiar?
No.

Why?
I thought it was a usual formality in crossing the border.

And next?
We crossed the border.

At night?
Yes

What happened?
Nothing.

Didn't you show a passport?
No, I didn't have one.

Didn't you think that peculiar?

No because I thought all this was arranged because the man sitting beside the driver handed out a paper and the guard waved them.

Next?
We drove on to a fort.

What name?
I can't remember. Fig something other.

Figueras?
Something like that, yes I suppose it was.

And then?
I fell ill.

What with?
A fever of some kind.

And then?
I didn't want to leave the rest of the English so I got on a train and don't remember anything else till I woke in a hospital in Barcelona.

What hospital?
Hospital Military I think.

Hospital Militar, eh?
Yes, I think so.

Didn't you think that was peculiar?
No, not until I began to get better.

When was that?
About ten days.

What did you think then?
That all the hospitals were full of wounded from Majorca.

Why did you think that?
Because I heard that name repeated in conversation and thought all civil hospitals had been commandeered.

Yes and then?
I went to Albacete.

Yes, but before you went what impression did you get of Barcelona?

What do you mean by that?

Well, did you see lots of drunkenness? Men with rifles on the street shouting songs, food queues or anything like that?
Well I was only out in the city on the road to the station and various offices for tickets, but I did see long queues of women

What for?
I don't know.

Where were these offices? And what were their names?
I don't know but I got a ticket and four other papers to get to Albacete.

Yes and how did you get there?
Through Valencia.

And then?
I went on to Madrigueras.

What did you do there?
Well I was put on sanitary work, digging holes and cleaning lavatories etc.

Then?
I realised I was in the army and decided to make the best of it.

What drill did you do?
I don't know.

What do you mean?
Well it seemed just senseless walking over ploughed fields.

Did you have rifles and rifle practice?
The last week we were there were issued rifles and lots of us fired five bullets each.

No more than that?
No

Why?
I don't know.

Who was in charge of you?
Do you mean the Battalion?

Yes

A man called McCartney

Did he write a book called *Walls have Mouths*?
I don't know.

Who was Wintringham?
I don't know but he spoke about war to us one night. Some of the boys thought he was an expert on war

Was he?
I don't know anything about war but I'm sure he wasn't.

Why?
Because he didn't seem to have any idea about things when we went into battle.

Did you have machine guns there?
No

Where did you get them?
In a town we arrived at when we left Madrigueras

What was its name?
I don't know.

Villajubia?
Villa something or other

What happened there?
We went up to the front

What kind of machine guns were they?
I don't know.

What kind of rifles?
I don't know.

Were they Russian?
I don't know but I remember at one time hearing they were Mexican.

What happened at the front?
We went up behind a pile of stones like a wall

Yes and then?
We just stayed there.

Who was in charge?
Dickson.

What happened to Dickson?
I don't know.

What did you do behind the wall?
We stayed there until dark.

Did you use your rifles?
Well, I tried to but the first time I fired it flew up into my face and I only used it when I thought anybody was looking.

In the morning did you use your rifle?
A little but I was not very anxious to get a kick in the face.

What happened next?
Until 4 a.m. we did nothing because of your artillery fire.

And then?
Well, a bunch of soldiers appeared above the crest of the slope about 10 yards ahead of us and we saw they were from the other side and we threw our rifles down to give them confidence and called them over.

What happened next?
Well they came over and said something and motioned to where they had come from and we followed them

Was there any trouble?
All the fellows didn't come out for work, some of them refused to throw down their rifles and were shot

Yes and then what?
We went down the slope and went to a town where we spent the night

What town?
I don't know. It was dark.

What happened then?
A priest came in who could speak English and questioned us about our surrender and we told him we came for work and decided to escape at the first opportunity.

Then?

We went to another town where we were put in cells and questioned.

What happened there?
Next we were taken to Talavera.

How were you treated there?
There was a certain amount of excitement in that town but considering it was war time we didn't do so badly. We are still here.

How was the discipline on the other side?
There was none.

What do you mean?
We didn't have any kind of order – one day one man in charge then another then another. It was like a mad house.

Who do you think will win?
If discipline means anything, there's only one horse in the race

What was the food like?
There isn't any, the last three days there seems to have been a great shortage.

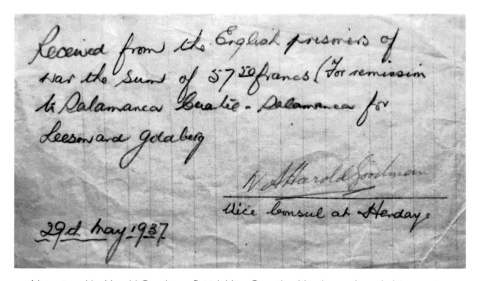

Note signed by Harold Goodman, British Vice-Consul at Hendaye, acknowledging receipt of money from the prisoners for the release of their comrades George Leeson & Maurice Goldberg, who had been detained in Salamanca.

After the interviews, Don Pablo Merry del Val told them that they had one last chance to save themselves from being shot dead, which was to fight on the fascist side. Each comrade remained silent.

They were put on trial and found guilty of 'aiding a military rebellion'. Five were sentenced to death, the Commander Harold Fry, plus George Leeson, Maurice Goldberg, Jimmy Rutherford and Charlie West, who was AC's best friend. The remaining men were all sentenced to 20 years' imprisonment.

As it turned out, none of the prisoners were executed at Salamanca. In May 1937 they were informed that Franco had pardoned them, the reason being that they were to be exchanged for a similar number of Italian prisoners captured by the Republican forces. They were exchanged and marched across the border at Irun into France, through a jeering aggressive crowd of fascist supporters with their hands raised in fascist style salute.

Most of the volunteers reached England by the end of May 1937. Jane

FRANCO CAPTIVES LAND IN LONDON

TWENTY-THREE Britons, over three months prisoners of Franco, returned to England yesterday, not freed by any feeling of mercy on the Fascists' part, but exchanged for prisoners on the Government side.

When they landed at Victoria Station at 6.15 p.m. they were met by D. F. Springhall and Peter Kerrigan, leaders of the London and Scottish Communist Parties respectively. A cheering crowd had also gathered to greet the gallant little band of anti-Fascists who since February have been living hour by hour under threat of death.

Three months of captivity had left its mark plainly on them. They cheered and grinned, but, like Arthur Koestler on his release, there was a tense, drawn look on their faces which told its own story.

All 23 were captured at San Martina, on the Madrid front, while serving in the Saklatvala Battalion of the International Brigade.

Five were sentenced to death, but had their sentences commuted. All were then imprisoned, under conditions which they describe as terrible beyond words.

They were left practically to starve, were forced to sleep on the ground with no straw or any

covers, and had no chance during all these months of having a proper wash.

Almost all fell ill with fever. Many prisoners contracted lung trouble, of which ten died.

Two of their own number were still in Talavera, so ill that they were unable to leave hospital.

TWO RETAINED

It had been arranged that 25 Britons should be released. At the last minute, however, two, Harold Leeson and Maurice Goldberg, were taken back into prison, "for some unknown reason."

Just before leaving Spain the Fascists arranged a farcical ceremony, in which John Stuhldreer, of Tottenham, was forced to shout "Viva Espana" into a microphone, and to "thank" Franco for his "generosity."

It was as bad a radio performance as there has ever been, the lads say with satisfaction.

Among the men who landed yesterday were Archibald Williams, Portsmouth, whose wife, a delegate to the Communist Party Congress, was at the station to meet him; Charles West, Mitcham; John Stuhldreer, Tottenham; Alfred Chowney, Sendmarsh, Surrey; Austin Skempton, East Molesey, and Basil Minsk, Mile End Road, East London.

A press report of the 23 British prisoners of Franco arriving at Victoria Station.

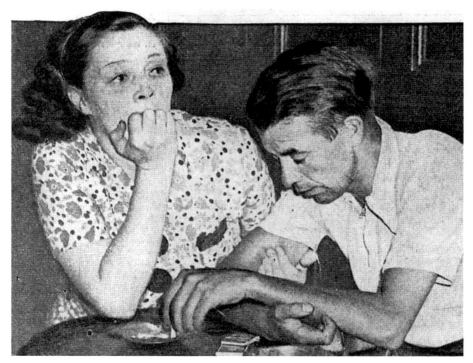

Jane Orme and AC pictured in the *Daily Herald* on Monday 31 May 1937, under the headline 'Spanish Fighter Meets Wife Again'. The paper describes Jane Orme's expression as 'eloquent in its silent appeal' after 'months of anxious waiting'.

Orme was at Victoria Station in London to meet her husband. She hardly recognised him, he was so thin and his hair was cropped to the scalp, which was covered in sores.

They were jubilantly reunited. In the waiting taxi with their friend Aunt Polly was their two-month-old baby girl, Rosemary Nina Williams, my mother.

Two of their party, Leeson and Goldberg were detained, possibly due to their Jewish sounding names, and their comrades campaigned for their release. AC told the press: 'There have been reports that we shouted "Long Live Franco". Not on your life!'

AC meeting his baby Rosemary, born when he was imprisoned in Spain.

After Spain

Back from war in Spain, AC was emaciated and traumatised, yet freedom-elated and overcome with emotion at being reunited with his wife of only a year and his tiny, doll-sized baby daughter. He'd witnessed many harrowing scenes in Spain during the five and half months he'd been there. The war was to rage for a further year. The crushing might of Franco's fascists continued in its destruction of the citizens who opposed him. AC and his wife could now enjoy the ordinary yet special pleasures of being new parents. Those hazy summer days in Hampshire and Sussex were a precious time for AC, his first taste of family life for decades.

A short holiday was arranged by Marjorie Pollitt, wife of Harry, the British Communist Party Leader. With his friend and fellow prisoner in Talavera, Charlie West, the two families travelled to the Gower in South Wales as the guests of Professor Farrington, who was lecturer in Classics at Swansea University, a communist and supporter of the International Brigade.

AC soon secured employment, firstly at Wellworthy Piston Rings Ltd in Lymington, alongside Charlie; followed by his appointment as manager of the Portsmouth branch of the Left Bookshop in Sultan Road which promoted 'Left Book Club' publications, set up to educate the British Left.

AC became the Communist Party's Literature Agent for Hampshire and Dorset.

In May 1938 another daughter was born, Jennifer <u>Talavera</u> Williams. Named to commemorate the comradeship in the prison at Talavera, she was never to forget the bravery of those imprisoned in the place she was named after in poor broken Spain.

During this time AC and Jane Orme were involved with the Aid Spain movement at Southampton, helping settle the 'ninõs', a group of almost 4,000 children who were evacuated from Bilbao in the Basque region. Two young children came to stay with the family when their daughters were young.

AC and Jane Orme were under the scrutiny of MI5. Their flat above the Left Bookshop in Portsmouth was raided and their personal papers stolen, including the manuscript of a book they had been writing together called 'Between Two Prison Gates'. Over the past 20 years, my family have tried to recover this precious work, which gives AC's account of his time in Canadian and Spanish jails and his experiences in between, but our enquiries have been fruitless. The explanation given is that it was destroyed long ago.

During the Second Word War, Whitehall maintained their 'tabs' on AC in a surprisingly direct way: they employed him! He was interviewed and offered the job of Labour Manager at one of the Royal Ordnance factories making ammunition in Euxton in the Borough of Chorley, Lancashire. Later he discovered other comrades that fought in Spain were similarly employed. It was then that AC was made to withdraw his membership of the Communist Party, with secure wartime employment and a tied house being the bargaining tool. He had very little choice but to accept the offer.

Their home was a newly constructed tiny 'prefab' kit house in Ryden Avenue, Leyland, and they loved it. Their Lancashire neighbours welcomed them warmly, along with the many other new families, all from different parts of the country, with their varied accents. Some were intellectuals, some also under scrutiny of MI5. None of the new neighbours' accents were as posh sounding as Jane Orme's, though on which neighbours commented.

Although a staunch socialist, she was brought up with polished, upper-class vowels. However, Rosemary and Jennifer quickly became broad-speaking Lancashire lasses and from their happy post-war childhood memories it seems like a golden era of neighbourly friendliness.

The small prefab gardens were just big enough to grow vegetables or keep livestock. AC was a good gardener but would never grow turnips as they had been his staple diet in the Spanish jail and the taste made him feel sick, remembering the rotten roots he had no choice but eat.

A shortage of homes in Leyland meant that the more quickly built prefabricated houses were constructed on land behind their house. The family were surprised to hear that the labourers who started to put in the new footings for the dwellings were German prisoners of war. At first people were wary but their children soon became friendly with the young men. Jane Orme and AC welcomed them into their home, inviting a group to have tea; my mum remembers their sad faces and their shaky hands when holding their cutlery. When they had finally finished at the site, they repaid the family with generous gifts of beautifully carved wooden boxes, fashioned during their time in the camps.

AC was a popular figure in the neighbourhood and also during his employment in the Royal Ordnance factory, where he successfully introduced an apprentice scheme that included training and education as well as implementing new Health and Safety standards, desperately needed in such a dangerous industry. He was focused on being a mentor to young

apprentices – he also taught them the quickstep and waltz and to jive!
AC's daughter Rosemary recalls:

Dad never talked about his role in Spain as an International
Brigader but he and Mum often spoke to each other in Spanish
so we could not understand their private chats. We got to know
certain phrases such as *dinero* (money) being discussed. Later
our Mum spoke briefly to my sister and I, stating that Dad was
traumatised after witnessing the horrors of battle, capture and
imprisonment in Spain. We were told by her that his friend
was shot at point-blank range and also that Dad and his fellow
prisoners were paraded out to stand in a firing squad and shots
were fired above the heads of some while others were shot dead.

We knew that he had some sort of breakdown when we were
young and he went to stay for a few weeks to recover in the Lake
District at Hill of Oaks on Windermere which aided his recovery.

Dad was a very friendly and honest person, much admired in
our Leyland neighbourhood. Rather than tell us depressing and
terrifying tales of his past, he preferred to share with us exciting
stories of his time in Canada and America as a young man.
However, he got angry talking about the Canadian Mounties, who
he described as being terrible brutes.

I remember him entertaining a large group of children during
playtime with his stories. When he sat upon an air raid shelter in the
playground of Farington Primary school in Leyland, he told of his
adventures as a lumberjack, rancher and fur trapper, and his love for
his horse, Blackie, who was so intelligent that it knew when there
was dangerous ice ahead. The school lunch bell rang and children
were so enraptured they were late for their afternoon class.

He taught my sister Jen and me to ride, showing us his cowboy
style of riding with long reigns and low stirrups. He would also
demonstrate using a lasso. He was a wonderful dancer and as a
young teenager I accompanied him with a few of my friends to a
dance class he held for his young male apprentices – we were to be
their partners. He led the instructions and rather than demonstrate
a stuffy tea-dance style, he showed us the fast moves of the
exciting Charleston and Jitterbug. We were also surprised that he

Rosemary Nina (left) and Jennifer Talavera Williams (right).

could play beautiful Highland dance tunes on a fiddle. During the war and the following years, Dad was still a labour manager at the Royal Ordnance factory between Leyland and Chorley, a few miles from our house. He was the main parent in our lives which was unusual for that era; he cooked, laundered, ironed and helped with our homework. Some of the neighbours felt sorry for him but he just laughed. It was Mum who was the activist then, always away from home at Hospital Management Committees in the early days of the National Health Service.

In Preston she set up a Citizens Advice Bureau and Marriage Guidance in two rooms above a butcher's shop. Due to pressure of long queues, which annoyed neighbouring offices and shops, she then was offered ground floor accommodation, an entrance hall with three large interview offices, to assist those with various problems and to enable her to organise interviews. Many activities took her away from the home, including public speaking or Soroptimists meetings. When she was at home, we were often told not to interrupt her as she typed her columns for the *News Chronicle* and *Lancashire Evening Post*. Dad supported her in these activities.

It's only in recent years that I found out the full facts of my dad's experiences in Spain due to my daughter's research. This included a remarkable trip to Spain. We visited Jarama and saw the exact spot where my dad was captured during the battle which was an overwhelming and emotional day, leaving me in tears of sorrow and pride.

As Rosemary mentions, her mother was involved with causes close to her heart. On a visit to an old army training camp in Adlington near Chorley, which housed Spanish Republican internees who had escaped from Spain, she interviewed the men and wrote articles about them for the *News Chronicle* with her well-known artist neighbour and friend Bob Mortimer sketching their portraits, which impressed everyone there. These men could not return to their home country – Franco's Spain – as they would have been tortured or murdered due to their opposition to the dictatorship. The British Labour Government for some reason did return some of the men to Spain, resulting in certain death or internment in a concentration camp.

My grandmother's *News Chronicle* article helped to highlight their plight, along with the 'Aid Spain' movement and the 'International Brigade Trust'. Later some of the men married local women and stayed in Lancashire.

In 1953, after years of living in a close community and forming many friendships, AC took work at another Royal Ordnance factory in Swynnerton, Staffordshire, and the family were rehoused in Stone, a nearby town.

Rosemary attended the local grammar school and Jennifer left home for an apprenticeship in hunt stables. When the Staffordshire plant closed, AC helped to find new positions for the redundant employees before his move north.

In the early 1960s AC's job took him to another Royal Ordnance factory, this time to Bishopton, in Renfrewshire, Scotland. Their next and final home was a cottage in lovely countryside at the bottom of a quiet country lane, in a small hamlet called Glenshinnoch, only two miles from Bishopton, bordering an unused area of the munitions factory land.

AC managed to rent the cottage for the both of them for many happy years. During this time, he was reunited with his brother Donald, whom he had not seen since they were teenagers. Donald was a print worker on the *Glasgow Herald* and visited their home on many occasions, with the brothers talking into the early hours. He printed out a newspaper called the *Glenshinnoch Gazette* written by AC and filled with his news, to be sent to his daughters Rosemary, Jennifer and the grandchildren. The 'news' included how many deer he had seen that day and details of collecting good wood for their fire from the nearby River Clyde shore. I remember as a child the visits from some of his old comrades, some wearing a beret and greeting one another with clenched fist salutes.

AC and Jane Orme were wonderful grandparents to my brothers and myself. Much warmth and fun was bestowed on us grandchildren on countless

happy holidays at their Scottish country cottage home. They inspired us with their knowledge and showered companionable love upon us – four noisy, scruffy, questioning children with an insatiable appetite to learn. They had a wealth of life experience that they shared passionately with us, educating each of us in the varied ways of their world, whether bird and flower identification, poetry, stories, woodcraft skills and cookery or living history lessons. No classroom could teach a child what we soaked up effortlessly,

AC at home in Renfrewshire 1970, aged 65.   clamouring for more.

AC and Jane Orme were spied on throughout their lives by the security services and through his government job and tied cottage he was totally politically compromised. It was an unexpected surprise to them both when, in the mid-1960s, MI5 contacted them to inform them that they were to attend a meeting in Whitehall, an invitation which they were not allowed to refuse. They were interrogated for a few hours including about their political beliefs. Jane Orme had early symptoms of Parkinson's disease and her hands often shook, as an officer noticed while she had a teacup in her hand and asked if she had something to hide. At this AC and Jane Orme both burst out laughing and they were sent on their way!

No. 2 Machine Gun Company

This book is about four members of No. 2 Machine Gun Company of the British Battalion of the xv International Brigade but it would not be complete without the names of their comrades, listed below. This information was sourced by Lisa Croft and Tam Watters from the International Brigade Memorial Trust, with additional assistance from Richard Baxell and Alan Warren. The IBMT website is an invaluable resource for activities and events commemorating the volunteers: www.international-brigades.org.uk

Comrades in prison & released May 1937

Abrahams, Basil (or Basil/David Minsk), London
Bloomfield, Thomas, Kirkcaldy
Chowney, Alfred, Woking
Flynn, Jack, London
Fry, Harold, Edinburgh
Giles, Stanley, Liverpool
Goldberg, Maurice, South Africa (Released later)
Hunter, John, Leith
Johnson, William,Seaton Deleval, Northumberland
Jones, Fred, Liverpool
Leeson, George, London (Born in Clonakilty, Ireland) (Released later)
Levy, Bert (or Yank), Windsor, Ontario
Maley, James, Glasgow
Martinson, Charles,Bootle (Released later from, hospital in Spain)
Montgomery, John, Glasgow
Payne, Richard C, London
Pugh, James, Liverpool
Renton, Donald, Portobello, Edinburgh
Rutherford, James, Leith
Silcock, Robert, Liverpool (Released later from hospital in Spain)
Skempton, Austin, East Moseley, Surrey
Stuhldeer, George, London
Thomas, Bernard D, Birmingham
Watters, George, Prestonpans
West, Charles, London
Wiffen, Grenville, Wirral
Williams, AC Mc, Portsmouth

Other members of No. 2 Machine Gun Company
(not imprisoned at Jarama)

Killed in action

Ball, William
Bibby, Leonard
Carter, Thomas
Gilmour, John (Jock)
Gold, Alfred (cook)
Katsaronas, Panayiotis (Cyprus: cabinet maker)
Lomax, Richard
Shields, Joseph (died from wounds in hospital)

Shot on capture

Dickenson, Ted (Australia)
Ellis (aka Elias), Phil
Silcock, Thomas
Stevens, John

Wounded/survived (some repatriated, some in further action)
*name not conclusive

Bodker, T
Blood, Edwin
Bruce, John
Casey, Francis (cook)
Doyle, P
Edelmann, Sidney
Ellis, Jack
Fleming, Robert
Galloway, Alan
Garber, Joseph
Hepper, Thomas*
Horbury, Harold
Hornsby, George
Johnston, William
Kirkpatrick, John (cook)
Keegan, William
Leat, George (cook)
Lewis, Paul
Martin, Peter*

Mclennan, James* (cook)
O'Neill, Charles*
Pugh, William
Sexton,Cyril
Silvermann, Alec (cook)
Vincent, S

Further Reading

The literature of the Spanish Civil War and its aftermath is vast. This list offers a selection of key historical works, including accounts of Scottish International Brigaders, the testimony of other internationalists who went to fight for the Republic, and other important eyewitness accounts.

Bill Alexander, *British Volunteers for Liberty: Spain 1936–1939* (London: Lawrence and Wishart, 1982).

Mike Arnott, *Dundee and the Spanish Civil War* (Dundee: Dundee Trades Union Council, 2008).

Ralph Bates, 'Of Legendary Time', *The Virginia Quarterly Review* 15, 1 (1939): 21–36.

Richard Baxell, *British Volunteers in the Spanish Civil War* (Pontypool: Warren & Pell, 2007).

Richard Baxell, 'Mac Paps', In *History Workshop Journal* 68, 1 (2009): 251–259.

Richard Baxell, Angela Jackson and Jim Jump, *Antifascistas: British and Irish Volunteers in the Spanish Civil War* (London: Lawrence & Wishart, 2010).

Richard Baxell, 'Myths of the International Brigades', *Bulletin of Spanish Studies* 91, 1–2 (2014): 11–24.

Antony Beevor, *The Battle for Spain* (London: Weidenfeld & Nicolson, 2006).

Gerald Brenan, *The Spanish Labyrinth: An Account of the Social and Political Background of the Spanish Civil War* (Cambridge: Cambridge University Press, 2014).

Lorne Brown, *When Freedom was Lost: The Unemployed, the Agitator and the State* (Montréal: Black Rose Books, 1987).

Tom Buchanan, *Britain and the Spanish Civil War* (Cambridge: Cambridge University Press, 1997).

Tom Buchanan, *The Spanish Civil War and the British Labour Movement* (Cambridge: Cambridge University Press, 2012).

Henry Buckley, *The Life and Death of the Spanish Republic: A Witness to the Spanish Civil War*, with an introduction by Paul Preston (London: I. B. Tauris, 2021; first published 1940).

Liam Cahill, *From Suir to Jarama: Mossie Quinlan's Life and Legacy* (Cork: Orla Kelly Publishing, 2021).

Peter Carroll, 'Psychology & Ideology in the Spanish Civil War: The Case of the Abraham Lincoln Brigade', *The Antioch Review* 52, 2 (1994): 219–230.

Julian Casanova, *The Spanish Republic and Civil War* (Cambridge: Cambridge University Press, 2010).

Stuart Christie, *Granny Made Me an Anarchist: General Franco, The Angry Brigade and Me* (Edinburgh: AK Press, 2007).

Danny Duncan Collum (ed.), *African Americans in the Spanish Civil War: 'This Ain't Ethiopia, but It'll Do'* (New York: GK Hall & Company, 1991).

Bob Cooney, *Proud Journey: A Spanish Civil War Memoir*, with Introduction by Meirian Jump (London: Marx Memorial Library & Workers' School and Manifesto Press, 2015).

John Corcoran, '"Fighting the good fight": The Rev. Robert Martin Hilliard (1904–1937)', *Saothar* 31 (2006): 55–62

David Corkill and Stuart J. Rawnsley (eds.), *The Road to Spain: Anti-fascists at War, 1936–1939* (Dunfermline: Borderline, 1981).

Malcolm Cowley, 'Lament for the Abraham Lincoln Battalion', *The Sewanee Review* 92, 3 (1984): 331–347.

Allan Craig, *Incident at Jarama: A Legacy from the Spanish Civil War – The Eventful Life of a Glasgow Lad, as Influenced by the Loss of his Father in the Spanish Civil War* (Glasgow: Clydeside Press/Research Collections at Glasgow Caledonian University, 2010).

Ilana Crome, 'Leonard Crome MC: Former Pathologist, Fountain Hospital', *Psychiatric Bulletin* 26, 5 (2002): 199.

Len Crome, 'Walter (1897–1947): A Soldier in Spain', *History Workshop* 9 (1980): 116–128.

Richard Croucher, *We Refuse to Starve in Silence: A History of the Unemployed Workers Movement* (London: Lawrence and Wishart, 1986).

Daniel Czitrom, 'Volunteers for Liberty: Letters from Joe and Leo Gordon, Americans in Spain 1937–38', *The Massachusetts Review* 25, 3 (1984): 347–365.

Peter Darman, *Heroic Voices of the Spanish Civil War: Memories from the International Brigades* (London: New Holland Publishers Ltd, 2009).

David Deacon, *British News Media and the Spanish Civil War: Tomorrow May Be Too Late* (Edinburgh: Edinburgh University Press, 2008).

Pierre Delva and Pierre Fournier, 'Norman Bethune: Surgeon Extraordinary', *World Health Forum* 11, 4 (1990): 373–375.

Jean Deslauriers and Denis Goulet, 'The Medical Life of Henry Norman Bethune', Canadian Respiratory Journal 22, 6 (2015): e32–e42.

Chris Dolan, *An Anarchist's Story: The Life of Ethel MacDonald* (Edinburgh: Birlinn, 2009).

Bob Doyle, with Harry Owens, *Brigadista: An Irishman's Fight Against Fascism* (Blackrock, Co. Dublin : Currach Press, 2006).

Chris Ealham and Michael Richards (eds.), *The Splintering of Spain: Cultural History and the Spanish Civil War, 1936–1939* (Cambridge: Cambridge University Press, 2005).

Cecil D. Eby, *Comrades and Commissars: The Lincoln Battalion in the Spanish Civil War* (University Park, PA: Penn State Press, 2007).

Deirdre Finnerty, 'Telling Their "War Story": A Comparative Analysis of the Perceptions of British and Spanish Women Activists of their Experiences of the Spanish Civil War', in Patricia O'Byrne, Gabrielle Carty and Niamh Thornton (eds.), *Transcultural Encounters Amongst Women: Redrawing Boundaries in Hispanic and Lusophone Art, Literature and Film* (2010): 107–122.

Harry Fisher, *Comrades: Tales of a Brigadista in the Spanish Civil War*, with a foreword by Pete Seeger (Lincoln and London: University of Nebraska Press, 1998).

Donald H. Forbes, *Two Communist Brothers from Washington, New Hampshire and their Fight Against Fascism*, edited by Jennifer Forbes Minnichelli (Morrisville, North Carolina: Lulu Press 2013).

Hywel Francis, 'Welsh Miners and the Spanish Civil War', *Journal of Contemporary History* 5, 3 (1970): 177–191.

Hywel Francis, '"Say Nothing and Leave in the Middle of the Night": The Spanish Civil War Revisited', *History Workshop Journal* 32, 1 (1991): 69–76.

Jim Fyrth and Sally Alexander (eds.), *Women's Voices from the Spanish Civil War* (London: Lawrence & Wishart, 2008).

Tom Gallagher, 'Scottish Catholics and the British Left, 1918–1939', *Innes Review* 34, 1 (1983): 17–42.

Barbara A. Gannon, '"They Call Themselves Veterans": Civil War and Spanish War Veterans and the Complexities of Veteranhood', *Journal of the Civil War Era* 5, 4 (2015): 528–550.

Daniel Pastor García and Antonio R. Celada, 'The Victors Write History, the Vanquished Literature: Myth, Distortion and Truth in the XV Brigade', *Bulletin of Spanish Studies* 89, 7–8 (2012): 307–321.

Carl Geiser, *Prisoners of the Good Fight: The Spanish Civil War, 1936–1939*, with a preface by Robert G. Colodny (Westport, Conn.: Lawrence Hill & Co., 1986).

Carl Geiser, 'The Task My Generation Faced (1936–1945)', *Science & Society* 68, 3 (2004): 329–336.

Marvin E. Gettleman, 'Robert G. Colodny: The Struggle against Fascism at Home and Abroad', *Science & Society* 68, 3 (2004): 263–271.

Mark J. Gillespie, *When the Gorbals Fought Franco: The Story of J. J. Lynch, International Brigade Volunteer. Irishman. Glaswegian*, 2nd edition (n.p.: 2016).

Frank Graham, *The Battle of Jarama 1937: The Story of the British Battalion of the International Brigade's Baptism of Fire in the Spanish War* (Newcastle: Howe Brothers Ltd, 1987).

Frank Graham, *Battles of Brunete and the Aragon* (Newcastle upon Tyne: Frank Graham, 1999).

Helen Graham, *The Spanish Republic at War 1936–1939* (Cambridge: Cambridge University Press, 2002).

Helen Graham, 'The Spanish Civil War, 1936–2003: The Return of Republican Memory', *Science & Society* 68, 3 (2004): 313–328.

Helen Graham, *The War and Its Shadow: Spain's Civil War in Europe's Long Twentieth Century* (Brighton: Sussex Academic Press, 2012).

Daniel Gray, *Homage to Caledonia: Scotland and the Spanish Civil War* (Edinburgh: Luath Press, 2008).

Nan Green, *Spain Against Fascism 1936–39: Some Questions Answered* (London: History Group of the Communist Party, 1976).

Nan Green, *A Chronicle of Small Beer: The Memoirs of Nan Green*, ed. RJ Ellis (Nottingham: Trent Editions, 2004).

Lucía Pintado Gutiérrez and Alicia Castillo Villanueva (eds.), *New Approaches to Translation, Conflict and Memory: Narratives of the Spanish Civil War and the Dictatorship* (Houndmills, Basingstoke: Palgrave Macmillan, 2019).

Carmel Haden Guest (ed.), *David Guest: A Scientist Fights for Freedom (1911–1938), A Memoir* (London: Lawrence & Wishart Limited, 1939).

Jason Gurney, *Crusade in Spain* (London: Faber and Faber, 1974).

Larry Hannant, '"My God, are they sending women?": Three Canadian Women in the Spanish Civil War, 1936–1939', *Journal of the Canadian Historical Association/Revue de la Société historique du Canada* 15, 1 (2004): 153–176.

S. Manøe Hansen, 'An Emigrant Destiny', trans. Birgit Langhammer, *Canadian Ethnic Studies/ Etudes Ethniques au Canada* 19, 1 (1987): 96–117.

Josephine Herbst, *The Starched Blue Sky of Spain and Other Memoirs*, with an introduction by Diane Johnson (New York: HarperCollins, 1992).

Gina Herrmann, 'Voices of the Vanquished: Leftist Women and the Spanish Civil War', *Journal of Spanish Cultural Studies* 4, 1 (2003): 11–29.

Janette Higgins, *Fighting for Democracy: The True Story of Jim Higgins (1907–1982), A Canadian Activist in Spain's Civil War* (Altona, Manitoba: FriesenPress, 2020).

Victor Hoar, 'In Our Time: The Abraham Lincoln Brigade and the Historians', *American Quarterly* 22, 1 (1970): 112–119.

James K. Hopkins, *Into the Heart of the Fire: The British in the Spanish Civil War* (Stanford, CA: Stanford University Press, 1998).

Ben Hughes, *They Shall Not Pass!: The British Battalion at Jarama* (Oxford: Osprey Publishing, 2011).

Dolores Ibárruri, *They Shall Not Pass: The Autobiography of La Pasionaria* (International Publishers Co, 1966).

Michael W. Jackson, 'The Army of Strangers: The International Brigades in the Spanish Civil War', *Australian Journal of Politics & History* 32, 1 (1986): 105–118.

Sarah Jackson, 'The British International Brigades as Labour Party Dissidents', *International Journal of Iberian Studies* 18, 1 (2005): 3–21.

Frank Jellinek and George Orwell, *The Civil War in Spain* (London: Gollancz, 1938).

Jim Jump (ed.), *Looking Back at the Spanish Civil War* (London: Lawrence & Wishart, 2010).

Jim Jump (ed.), *Poets from Spain: British and Irish International Brigaders on the Spanish Civil War* (London: Lawrence & Wishart, 2006).

Judith Keene, 'A Spanish Springtime: Aileen Palmer and the Spanish Civil War', *Labour History* 52 (1987): 75–87.

Victor Kiernan, 'Labour and the War in Spain', *Scottish Labour History Society Journal* 11 (1977): 4–16.

Lisa A. Kirschenbaum, *International Communism and the Spanish Civil War: Solidarity and Suspicion* (Cambridge: Cambridge University Press, 2015).

H. Gustav Klaus (ed.), *Strong Words, Brave Deeds: The Poetry, Life and Times of Thomas O'Brien, Volunteer in the Spanish Civil War* (The O'Brien Press: Dublin, 1994).

Arthur Koestler, *Spanish Testament* (London: Gollancz, 1937).

Jan Kurzke, *The Good Comrade: Memoirs of an International Brigader* (London: Clapton Press, 2021).

Ben Leider, 'Last Letters from Spain', *Current History and Forum* 46, 1 (1937): 46.

Allan E. Levine, 'Levy, Bert "Yank" (05 October 1897–02 September 1965), Soldier and Writer', *American National Biography*, accessed 8 November 2021.

Laurie E. Levinger, *Love and Revolutionary Greetings: An Ohio Boy in the Spanish Civil War* (Benton, Searcy, Arkansas: Resource Publications, 2012).

'Yank' Bert Levy, *Guerrilla Warfare*, with an introduction by Franklin Mark Osanka (Boulder, Colorado: Paladin Press, 1964).

Lisa Lines, 'Female Combatants in the Spanish Civil War: *Milicianas* on the

Front Lines and in the Rearguard', *Journal of International Women's Studies* 10, 4 (2009): 168–187.

Eunice Lipton, *A Distant Heartbeat: A War, a Disappearance, and a Family's Secrets* (Albuquerque: University of New Mexico Press 2016).

Ronald Liversedge, *Mac–Pap: Memoir of a Canadian in the Spanish Civil War, edited by David Yorke* (Vancouver: New Star Books, 2013).

John Maley and Willy Maley, *From The Calton to Catalonia* (Glasgow: Calton Books, 2014; first published Clydeside Press, 1993).

Shirley Mangini, 'Memories of Resistance: Women Activists from the Spanish Civil War', *Signs* 17, 1 (1991): 171–186.

Jorge Marco and Peter Anderson, 'Legitimacy by Proxy: Searching for a Usable Past through the International Brigades in Spain's Post–Franco Democracy, 1975–2015', *Journal of Modern European History* 14, 3 (2016): 391–410.

Jorge Marco and Maria Thomas, '"Mucho malo for fascisti": Languages and Transnational Soldiers in the Spanish Civil War', *War & Society* 38, 2 (2019): 139–161.

Andrew Pierre Marty, *Heroic Spain* (Toronto: New Era Publishers, 1937).

Lewis Mates, *The Spanish Civil War and the British Left: Political Activism and the Popular Front* (London: Bloomsbury Publishing, 2007).

John McGovern, *Why Bishops Back Franco: Report of Visit of Investigation to Spain* (London: Independent Labour Party, 1936).

Josie McLellan, 'The Politics of Communist Biography: Alfred Kantorowicz and the Spanish Civil War', *German History* 22, 4 (2004): 536–562.

Josie McLellan, '"I Wanted to be a Little Lenin": Ideology and the German International Brigade Volunteers', *Journal of Contemporary History* 41, 2 (2006): 287–304.

Jim McNeill, 'Ted Dickinson: Profile', *Australian Left Review* 1, 4 (1966): 41–45.

Donald L. Miller, 'Fighting In Spain: A Conversation With Steve Nelson', *Salmagundi* 76/77 (1987–1988): 113–132.

Myron Momryk, '"For Your Freedom and For Ours": Konstantin (Mike) Olynyk, A Ukrainian Volunteer From Canada in the International Brigades', *Canadian Ethnic Studies/Etudes Ethniques au Canada* 20, 2 (1988): 124–134.

Joe Monks, *With the Reds in Andalusia* (London: The John Cornford Poetry Group, 1985).

Cary Nelson and Jefferson Hendricks (eds.), *Madrid 1937: Letters of the Abraham Lincoln Brigade From the Spanish Civil War* (London: Routledge, 1996).

Joseph North, *Men in the Ranks: The Story of 12 Americans in Spain*, with a foreword by Ernest Hemingway (New York: Friends of the Abraham Lincoln Brigade, 1939).

Peadar O'Donnell, *Salud! An Irishman in Spain* (London: Methuen, 1937).

Joseph O'Connor, Even The Olives Are Bleeding: The Life and Times of Charles Donnelly (Dublin: New island Books, 1992).

Antonio Ramos Oliveira, *The Drama of Spain: From the Proclamation of the Republic to the Civil War 1931–1936* (London: The National Council of Labour, 1936).

Michael O'Riordan, *The Connolly Column: The Story of the Irishmen who Fought for the Spanish Republic 1936–1939* (Dublin: New Books, 1979; Pontypool: Warren & Pell, 2005).

George Orwell, *Homage to Catalonia* (London: Penguin Classics, 2000; first published Secker & Warburg, 1938).

George Orwell, 'Looking Back on the Spanish War', Alex Comfort and John Bayliss (eds.), *New Road 1943: New Directions in Art and Letters* (Billericay, Essex: The Grey Walls Press, 1943).

Abe Osheroff, 'Reflections of a Civil War Veteran', in Janet Pérez and Wendell Aycock (eds.), *The Spanish Civil War in Literature* (Lubbock, Texas: Texas Tech University Press, 1990), 9–22.

Harry Owens, 'Memories of Defeat and Exile', *Bulletin of Spanish Studies* 91, 1–2 (2014): 199–226.

Linda Palfreeman, *Aristocrats, Adventurers and Ambulances: British Medical Units in the Spanish Civil War* (Eastbourne: Sussex Academic Press, 2014).

Margaret Palmer and Garnett McCoy, 'Letters from Spain 1936–1939', *Archives of American Art Journal* 26, 2/3 (1986): 2–20.

Frances Patai, 'Heroines of the Good Fight: Testimonies of US Volunteer Nurses in the Spanish Civil War, 1936–1939', Nursing History Review 3, 1 (1995): 79–104.

Stanley G Payne, *The Spanish Civil War* (Cambridge: Cambridge University Press, 2012).

E Allison Peers, 'A Diary of the Civil War in Spain', *Bulletin of Spanish Studies*, serialised from 13, 52 (1936): 177–182 to 15, 60 (1938): 232–238.

E Allison Peers, *Catalonia Infelix* (New York: Oxford University Press, 1938).

Michael Petrou, 'Canadian Volunteers in the Spanish Civil War: New Evidence from the Comintern Archives', *Labour/Le Travail* 56 (2005): 371–375.

Michael Petrou, *Renegades: Canadians in the Spanish Civil War* (Vancouver and Toronto: University of British Columbia Press Toronto, 2008).

Matthew Poggi, 'Saving Memories: Canadian Veterans of the Spanish

Civil War and Their Pursuit of Government Recognition', *American Communist History* 12, 3 (2013): 193–212.

Albert Prago, 'Jews in the International Brigades', *Jewish Currents* (February 1979): 15–21.

Albert Prago, Jews in the International Brigades: 2', *Jewish Currents* (March 1979): 6–9, 24–27.

Paul Preston, *!Comrades!: Portraits from the Spanish Civil War* (Glasgow: Fontana Press, 2000).

Paul Preston, *Doves of War: Four Women of Spain* (London: HarperCollins, 2002).

Paul Preston, *The Spanish Civil War: Reaction, Revolution & Revenge* (London: Harper Perennial, 2006).

Paul Preston, *We Saw Spain Die: Foreign Correspondents in the Spanish Civil War* (London: Constable, 2009; first published 2008).

Paul Preston, 'No Soldier: The Courage and Comradeship of Dr Len Crome', in Jim Jump (ed.), *Looking Back at the Spanish Civil War* (London: Lawrence & Wishart, 2010), 31–44.

Paul Preston, *The Spanish Holocaust: Inquisition and Extermination in Twentieth-Century Spain* (London: HarperPress, 2012).

Paul Preston, 'Two Doctors and One Cause: Len Crome and Reginald Saxton in the International Brigades', *International Journal of Iberian Studies* 19, 1 (2006): 5–24.

Fraser Raeburn, *Scots and the Spanish Civil War: Solidarity, Activism and Humanitarianism* (Edinburgh: Edinburgh University Press, 2021).

Fraser Raeburn, '"The Surest of All Morale Barometers": Transnational Encounters in the xv International Brigade', *Contemporary European History* (2021): 1–15, doi:10.1017/S0960777321000217.

Scott Ramsay, 'Salamanca, May 1937: The Eighth Marquis del Moral and the Turning Point in General Franco's Foreign Policy Towards Great Britain in the Spanish Civil War', *Bulletin of Spanish Studies* (2021): https://doi.org/10.1080/14753820.2021.1971863.

Michael Richards, *After the Civil War: Making Memory and Re-Making Spain since 1936* (Cambridge: Cambridge University Press, 2013).

Barbara Roberts, *Whence They Came: Deportation from Canada, 1900–1935* (Ottawa: University of Ottawa, 1988).

Esmond Romilly, *Boadilla: A Personal Record of the English Group of the Thaelmann Battalion of the International Brigade in Spain* (London: Hamish Hamilton, 1937).

Robert A Rosenstone, 'The Men of the Abraham Lincoln Battalion', *The Journal of American History* 54, 2 (1967): 327–338.

Julius Ruiz, 'Defending the Republic: The García Atadell Brigade in Madrid,

1936', *Journal of Contemporary History* 42, 1 (2007): 97–115.

William Rust, *Britons in Spain: The History of the British Battalion of the XVth International Brigade* (London: Lawrence & Wishart, 1939).

Tim Scheffe, 'Hints of Heroism, Traces of Trauma: Trauma and Narrative Structure in Interviews with Dutch and English International Brigade Volunteers of the Spanish Civil War', in Nanci Adler, Remco Ensel and Michael Wintle (eds.), *Narratives of War: Remembering and Chronicling Battle in Twentieth-Century Europe* (New York: Routledge, 2019), 163–179.

Hans A. Schmitt, 'The Spanish Civil War: Memories and Reassessments', *The Sewanee Review* 98, 2 (1990): 279–287.

Paul Schue, 'The Prodigal Sons of Communism: Parti Populaire Français Narratives of Communist Recruitment for the Spanish Civil War and the Everyday Functioning of Party Ideology', *French Historical Studies* 24, 1 (2001): 87–111.

Colin Shindler, 'No Pasaran: The Jews Who Fought in Spain', *Jewish Quarterly* 33, 3 (1986): 34–41.

Peggy Seigel, 'A Minister's Son, A Haunted Town, and the Spanish Civil War', *Indiana Magazine of History* 112, 2 (2016): 81–107.

Tony Shaw, '"Some Writers Are More Equal Than Others": George Orwell, the State and Cold War Privilege', *Cold War History* 4, 1 (2003): 143–170.

Najati Sidqi, 'I Went to Defend Jerusalem in Cordoba: Memoirs of a Palestinian Communist in the Spanish International Brigades', *Jerusalem Quarterly* 62 (2015): 102–109.

Pat Sloan (ed.), *John Cornford: A Memoir* (London: Jonathan Cape, 1938).

Eric Smith, 'Premature McCarthyism: Spanish Republican Aid and the Origins of Cold War Anti-Communism', in Robert Justin Goldstein (ed.), *Little 'Red Scares: Anti-Communism and Political Repression in the United States, 1921–1946* (London and New York: Routledge, 2016), 195–212.

John Sommerfield, *Volunteer in Spain* (London: Alfred Knopf, 1937).

H Rosi Song, 'Visual Fictions and the Archive of the Spanish Civil War', *Modern Language Notes* 129, 2 (2014): 367–390.

DP (Pat) Stephens, *A Memoir of the Spanish Civil War: An Armenian-Canadian in the Lincoln Battalion*, edited and with an Introduction by Rick Rennie (St John's, Newfoundland: Canadian Committee on Labour History, 2000).

Katharine Marjory Stewart–Murray, Duchess of Atholl, *Searchlight on Spain* (London: Penguin, 1938).

Rob Stradling, 'English–speaking Units of the International Brigades: War,

Politics and Discipline', *Journal of Contemporary History* 45, 4 (2010): 744–767.

Paul Philippou Strongos, *Spanish Thermopylae: Cypriot Volunteers in the Spanish Civil War, 1936–39* (Barcelona: Warren & Pell Publishing, 2009).

Brigitte Studer, *The Transnational World of the Cominternians*, trans. Dafydd Rees Roberts (Houndmills, Basingstoke: Palgrave Macmillan, 2015).

Fred A. Thomas, *To Tilt at Windmills: A Memoir of the Spanish Civil War* (East Lansing: Michigan State University Press, 1996).

Hugh Thomas, *The Spanish Civil War* (Harmondsworth: Penguin, 1965; first published 1961).

Giles Tremlett, *Ghosts of Spain: Travels Through Spain and Its Silent Past* (London: Faber, 2006).

Giles Tremlett, 'The Afterlives of the International Brigades', *History Today* (15 October 2020), https://www–historytoday–com.ezproxy.lib. gla.ac.uk/miscellanies/afterlives–international–brigades, accessed 20 November 2021.

Lise Vogel, 'Sidney Vogel: Spanish Civil War Surgeon', *American Journal of Public Health* 98, 12 (2008): 2147.

Irving Weissman, 'The Return', *The Massachusetts Review* 19, 3 (1978): 604–620.

Tyler Wentzell, 'Canada's Foreign Enlistment Act and the Spanish Civil War', *Labour /Le Travail* 80 (2017): 213–246.

George Wheeler, *To Make the People Smile Again: A Memoir of the Spanish Civil War*, edited by Jack Leach with a foreword by Jack Jones (Newcastle upon Tyne: Zymurgy Publishing, 2003).

John T. Whitaker, 'Prelude to World War: A Witness from Spain', *Foreign Affairs* 21, 1 (1942): 103–119.

Tom Wintringham, *English Captain* (London: Faber and Faber, 1939).

Gerben Zaagsma, *Jewish Volunteers, the International Brigades and the Spanish Civil War* (London: Bloomsbury Academic, 2017).

Acknowledgements

The authors wish to thank Gavin MacDougall and all at Luath Press for making this book possible.

Lisa Croft wishes to thank Alan Lloyd from Southampton, an active IBMT member who has researched International Brigaders from Hampshire. He supplied vital MI5 documents and interviews accessed from the National Archives at Kew and documents from the Marx Memorial Library. Thanks also to Michael Harrison who supplied newspaper articles relating to AC's time in Canada – in particular the unemployed worker riots and the Toronto bank fire. Above all, Lisa wishes to thank her mum Rosemary for the journey they made together, uncovering and illuminating many unknown aspects of AC's life – a joyful, sometimes upsetting but unforgettable shared experience.

Willy Maley would like to thank Conrad Wood and Craig Curran for the interviews they conducted with James Maley in 1991 and 2004, Dini Power for transcribing those interviews, Almudena Cros for help with images and MI5 for keeping scrupulous records of members of the Communist Party.

Jennie Renton would like to thank Jane Goldman and Gus McLean for their friendship and encouragement; Maddie Mankey for her sense of humour, skill and honesty; Owen Dudley Edwards for bringing to light her father's *Tribune* columns; Stuart MacLennan and the Scottish Labour History Society for permission to quote from Ian Wood's interview with Donald Renton (SLHS No. 11, 1977, Spanish Civil War issue); and William Lytle of Edinburgh Books for giving her first refusal on *XV International Brigade: Records of the British, American, Canadian and Irish Volunteers in Spain 1936–1936* (Madrid, 1938), which acted as a talisman.

Tam Watters would like to thank his daughter, Angela, for making him aware of the 'Scotland and the Spanish Civil War' Facebook page which commemorates the men who fought in the International Brigades; his son, Steven, for research which led to discovering that the Marx Memorial Library held a letter and photo that Ellen Watters sent to the International Brigades Dependants' Aid Committee in 1937; his brother, Jimmy, who helped out with his memories of events that occurred before Tam was born; and most of all his wife, Ishbel, who spent many months searching newspaper archives and RGASPI, the Moscow Archives.

Thanks to RGASPI for giving unlimited free access to anyone researching their files relating to the Spanish Civil War. Thanks to Prestonpans Labour Club for hosting several commemorative events paying tribute to the local men who fought in Spain. Thanks also to Alan Warren, Stuart Walsh and Mike Arnott who freely share their extensive knowledge of the Spanish Civil War in such a helpful manner on the International Brigades Facebook pages, and to Jim Jump, Richard Baxell and others, who do a great job with the International Brigades Memorial Trust. Finally, huge thanks to Robbie Gordon and Jack Nurse for writing and producing the excellent play *549: Scots of the Spanish Civil War* and to Mihaela Bodlovic for permission to reproduce her photographs of the play.

Also published by **LUATH PRESS**

Homage to Caledonia
Scotland and the Spanish Civil War
Daniel Gray
ISBN 978-1-913025-36-6 PBK £12.99

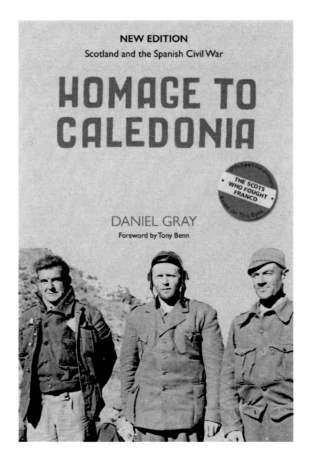

Daniel Gray's important and powerful book Homage to Caledonia
*tells the story of those deeply committed and courageous Scots who
volunteered to fight for democracy and socialism against General
Franco and his forces.*
TONY BENN

*Told through the words and experiences of those who were there, this
meticulously researched and beautifully written book is simultaneously
heart-breaking and uplifting.*
MAGGIE CRAIG

Details of books published by Luath Press can be found at:
www.luath.co.uk

Luath Press Limited

committed to publishing well written books worth reading

LUATH PRESS takes its name from Robert Burns, whose little collie Luath (*Gael.*, swift or nimble) tripped up Jean Armour at a wedding and gave him the chance to speak to the woman who was to be his wife and the abiding love of his life. Burns called one of the 'Twa Dogs' Luath after Cuchullin's hunting dog in Ossian's *Fingal*. Luath Press was established in 1981 in the heart of Burns country, and is now based a few steps up the road from Burns' first lodgings on Edinburgh's Royal Mile. Luath offers you distinctive writing with a hint of unexpected pleasures.

Most bookshops in the UK, the US, Canada, Australia, New Zealand and parts of Europe, either carry our books in stock or can order them for you. To order direct from us, please send a £sterling cheque, postal order, international money order or your credit card details (number, address of cardholder and expiry date) to us at the address below. Please add post and packing as follows: UK – £1.00 per delivery address; overseas surface mail – £2.50 per delivery address; overseas airmail – £3.50 for the first book to each delivery address, plus £1.00 for each additional book by airmail to the same address. If your order is a gift, we will happily enclose your card or message at no extra charge.

Luath Press Limited
543/2 Castlehill
The Royal Mile
Edinburgh EH1 2ND
Scotland
Telephone: 0131 225 4326 (24 hours)
Email: sales@luath.co.uk
Website: www.luath.co.uk